AMERICAN SOCIOLOGICAL HEGEMONY

Transnational Explorations

Dan A. Chekki
University of Winnipeg

UNIVERSITY
PRESS OF
AMERICA

Lanham • New York • London

T.S.

Copyright © 1987 by

University Press of America,® Inc.

4720 Boston Way
Lanham, MD 20706

3 Henrietta Street
London WC2E 8LU England

British Cataloging in Publication Information Available

Library of Congress Cataloging-in-Publication Data

Chekki, Danesh A.
American sociological hegemony.

Bibliography: p.
Includes index.
1. Sociology—United States—History—20th century.
2. Sociology—India—History—20th century.
3. Sociology—Canada—History—20th century.
4. Sociology—Cross-cultural studies.   I. Title.
HM22.U5C54   1987   301'.0973   87-18988
ISBN 0-8191-6611-1 (alk. paper)
ISBN 0-8191-6612-X (pbk. : alk. paper)

2-19-90

Dedicated

to my

Grandparents

ACKNOWLDEGEMENTS

I owe a debt of gratitude to Professor Kurt H. Wolff, Brandeis University, for reading a good many pages of a preliminary draft of this study and encouraging me to further explore some crucial issues in the sociology of knowledge.

Grateful acknowledgements are due to the administrators and colleagues at the University of Winnipeg who have facilitated my research endeavors. I wish to thank Doreen Smith for timely encouragement. Special thanks are due to Paul Redekop for his helpful comments on an earlier draft of this manuscript. My wife Sheela deserves recognition for her patience and familial responsibilities. This book is dedicated to the memory of my grandparents who supported my initial sociological adventures.

CONTENTS

PREFACE

It was more than thirty years ago that I was first exposed to Sociology. This initiation process took place primarily through American textbooks. In graduate school I read the works of Durkheim, Weber and many other European sociologists mostly through translations and introductions provided by American sociologists. In those days the writings of Karl Marx were considered more relevant to Economics, Politics and Philosophy rather than to Sociology. Most of the sociological journals that we could read were also American. During the 1950s a number of American social scientists came to the University of Bombay for research and/or teaching. This flow of American social scientists to many universities in India continued in the 1960s influencing the content and approach of teaching and trends in research as well.

When I began teaching sociology in the late 1950s in India most of the textbooks and supplementary readings were American. Again for research purposes, one could refer to a vast amount of sociological research literature produced in the United States. My experience of teaching and research in Canada since 1968 has further reinforced my earlier belief that American sociology plays a crucial role in contemporary global sociology. Physical proximity, cultural and economic dominance of the United States have tended to make sociology in America and in Anglophone Canada almost indistinguishable. This was the situation that prevailed in the 1960s at least. Since the 1970s sociologies in India and in Canada have been reacting to this hegemony of American sociology.

This book, following a 'sociology of sociology' and a 'sociology of knowledge' framework, attempts to provide a descriptive analysis of the nature, growth and diversity of American sociology and its predominant influence on the sociologies of India and Canada, especially after 1945. The first two chapters present an outline of sociology of sociology/ knowledge and identify a few questions and issues that need examination. The third chapter on American sociology aims to delineate the post war development of sociology and looks briefly at varieties of theories - paradigms, methodology and research. This chapter tries to focus upon the preeminent influence of American sociology abroad. The following chapters on India and Canada show the growth of national sociologies subject to the dominant influence of American sociology. Chapter six addresses the issue of fact-value controversy or objectivity - value commitment debate, or positivism/humanism dichotomy and considers the role of sociologists. Chapter seven examines the merits and limitations of national sociologies and problems and prospects of developing a sociology that transcends national boundaries. The concluding remarks make a strong plea for cross-national comparative research and the development of a universal sociology that is strongly supported by national sociologies. This comparative analyses of national sociologies, it is hoped, will illuminate the influence of socio-cultural forces within and across nations on the sociologies of the United States, India and Canada.

Is a universal science of sociology possible? What are the consequences of diverse national sociologies for developing a discipline of sociology that transcends national and/or cultural boundaries? Can sociology be nation-free? What is the future of sociology? What are the major roles sociologists play in their society? Is the sociologist a disinterested or sympathetic observer of society? Does the sociologist act as an academic critic, or as an advocate or activist involved in structural change? How do sources of financial support for research influence research priorities, methodology and theoretical orientations of sociologists? What are the ethical dilemmas encountered by sociologists? It also raises questions, such as: Sociology by whom?; for whom?; and most importantly, for what ends? These questions, addressed by some sociologists, demand further examination. This study attempts to provide an overview of the consensus and controversies that prevail around these issues.

The purpose of this book is not to present only a description and analyses of origin and development of sociology in the United States, India, and Canada. We already have such works. The primary focus of this volume, however, is to provide a synthetic descriptive comparative analyses of the influence of the sociocultural milieu on the development of sociologies in three countries; and more specifically to demonstrate the dominant influence of American sociology on the sociologies of India and Canada.

Although there is a need to explore in depth the complex interplay of scientific and ideological elements of these sociologies, I have resisted this temptation. Can sociology be a science altogether rather than the expression of a culture or a time? These aspects of the sociology of knowledge, I believe, should form a part of another study.

This work is a modest attempt to illustrate the central conceptions of sociology of knowledge, i.e., that all knowledge is socially constructed; what is accepted as a dominant ideology is the ideology of the elite group; there cannot be such a thing as a value-free science. So far, our efforts to make sociology a universal science have been sporadic and without profound achievements. Perhaps a realistic goal would be that sociologists should strive toward developing a universal scientific-humanistic sociology. This is not to say that the task is easy. But it is much worse to pretend that sociology is nothing but a science. The global village and spaceship earth concepts are now becoming a reality. Correspondingly, the need for global sociology is more pressing. I have advocated for an international sociology, and I hope that sociologists will make a concerted effort toward developing a strong international sociology.

DAN A. CHEKKI
University of
W i n n i p e g

CHAPTER I

SOCIAL CONTEXT OF SOCIOLOGY

Sociology is viewed by many sociologists as a scientific discipline;[1] and by some as a humanistic discipline. We would like to consider sociology as a scientific-humanistic discipline with a set of ideas, values, norms, a history, professional group of sociologists, and organizational forms. Sociologists are engaged in knowledge creation, transmission, and application. This seemingly universal discipline tends to vary in nature and content in different countries because of differences in socio-cultural contexts.

However, the perspectives of modern sociology represented in the United States of America, India, Canada, and in other countries do share certain common assumptions such as: the assumption that human behavior is learned, patterned, and repetitious; a common vocabulary of shared meanings and concepts for describing human behavior in different cultures; and a commitment to cross-cultural/cross-national generalizations about human relationships, groups, communities, social institutions, processes, problems, and societies without temporal or spatial limits.

Despite its aims and aspirations, sociology today is largely culture and nation-bound, reflecting the ideologies and problems of the country in which it is found. Therefore, it is necessary to understand the nature and content of national sociologies which are primarily derived from and responsive to their socio-economic, political and cultural milieu. In fact, sociological inquiry has always been related to the issues and problems characteristic of specific societies and time periods. For instance, modern sociology itself emerged in the efforts to grasp the problems of the French Revolution and the Industrial Revolution.

Sociology, though recognized as a scientific enterprise by many of its practitioners, is immersed in history.[2] Since society is an unfinished reality, the subject of sociological analysis is forever changing. Therefore, sociology is perpetually influenced by the transformation of the societies that it studies. Its observations are subject to varied interpretations by different groups of sociologists having a variety of ideological backgrounds.

Society is also a moral reality, and as such, sociological knowledge creation is influenced by the ethical context of the society and that of the sociologist's values. That is why sociology, it seems, cannot be completely isolated from becoming a subject of morality.

Moreover, sociology tends to modify social reality while studying it, and in turn society responds and reacts and is guided by them to varying degrees. In fact, different traditions in sociology, the plurality of tendencies and the diversity of ideologies[3] which have guided sociological theory and empirical research have been identified by sociologists.

Sociology, like all other disciplines, has been influenced by its national milieu and by the socio-economic background, ideology and professional training of its practitioners. What sociologists can do is influenced by the state of the art and by the changing needs and problems of society. Though sociology aspires to be a universal science, in reality it happens to be space and culture bound.

Every sociologist is born into a particular society and his/her perception and interpretation of reality has inescapably been shaped by the culture of that society. In this sense a sociologist is made, not born, and before one becomes a sociologist one is indelibly stamped with a culture. A sociologist's nationality, language, religion, region, social class, family, values, needs and priorities tends to influence the development of sociology. The ideological orientations of sociologists often provide the main elements of sociological perception of the problems that interest the sociologist, which in turn influence the way the sociologist conceptualizes and expresses these problems. As a consequence, sociology cannot exist completely outside the socio-cultural milieu of the sociologist. As a matter of fact, from its beginnings sociology has been intimately associated with nationality despite its goal of universal science.[4]

In other words, sociology as a body of knowledge cannot develop in a social vacuum. Sociology, as it is taught and practiced in a particular society, is largely a product of the complex socio-cultural system. Sociology, in this sense, happens to be the mirror[5] of the larger society in which it is practiced. Several scholars (Marx 1963, Mannheim 1936, Myrdal 1977, Wolff 1946, Mills 1959, Gouldner 1970, Friederichs 1970) have demonstrated that ideologies and value premises play an important role in sociological theorizing and research.

Furthermore, the socio-cultural system has a significant impact upon the investigator's methodologies and modes of

analysis.   The sociology of knowledge stresses this contextual
relativity of sociological thinking.

On the basis of the sociology of knowledge perspective
developed by Marx and Mannheim, contemporary sociologists such as
Merton and Coser suggest that the development of sociological
knowledge be related to the social, economic, and political
conditions of the society in which it emerges.   In contrast,
Parsons and Bierstedt believe that ideas are relatively autonomous
in the stream of history and are more dependent upon antecedent
ideas than they are upon the social, economic, or political
circumstances prevailing at the time of their appearance.

This study attempts to examine these viewpoints in light of
the growth and diffusion of American sociology in relation to its
socio-cultural milieu.   Furthermore, we examine the process of
institutionalization of sociology and socialization of
sociologists in India and in Canada.   The purpose of this analysis
is to show how sociologies in India and in Canada have not only
developed in response to their respective milieu but also have
been influenced by American sociology.

This comparative analysis of national sociologies is intended
to demonstrate the predominant influence of American sociology on
sociologies of India and Canada;   and their struggle for
independent identity.   The trend toward universalization of
sociology, in recent decades, seems to imply the acceptance of
American sociology which itself is said to be ethnocentric,
culture-bound, and parochial. In this context a question is often
raised: To what extent is American sociology relevant to
different national-cultural contexts of India and Canada?

This important question notwithstanding, it is our assumption
that American sociology has made a significant impact on the
sociologies of India and Canada during the post World War II
period.   Conversely, Indian and Canadian sociologies have not
influenced American sociology. As such, for the purpose of this
study we consider American sociology as a major force in shaping
Indian and Canadian sociologies.

Different models have been used to analyze the nature and
development of sociology in various countries.   For instance, the
institutional model considers sociology within the context of
educational institutions where university structures, traditions,
and rivalries influence the shape of the sociological enterprise
(Ben-David, Shils).

The ideological congruence model demonstrates the influence
of societal values and ideologies in the nature, conception and
development of sociology (Mannheim, Myrdal, Mills, Friedrichs,
Gouldner).

The contextual analysis model is intradisciplinary in its forms, and deals with the dominance, decline and fall of major paradigms, theoretical schools, shifts and conflicts, fads and fashions, leadership and control of intellectual means of production in sociology and other disciplines (Kuhn, Wiley, Mullins, Ritzer).

A dependency model has emerged on the basis of the conviction that the main centres of sociological dominance, power and prestige, and influence are located outside the boundaries of a national social science community (Lamy, Atal, Sharma, Loubser, Hiller). This external orientation is attributed to the underdevelopment of the internal disciplinary community. There is a growing concern expressed in terms of the 'vertical' relationship between social scientists in Europe and North America and those in the Third World; the dependency of the latter upon the former. There is implicit recognition of intellectual imperialism and neo-colonial exploitation involved. This academic intellectual imperialism is not only characteristic of the kind of dependency relations characteristic of the Third World but also between the United States and Canada as well as between America and Australia and a few other industrialized countries.

In the context of dependency theory and world system theory, American sociology forms the "core", whereas the sociologies of India and Canada tend to be associated with the "peripheral" and/or "semi- peripheral" units in a system of global sociology.

In terms of economic and political power and consequent hegemonic influences of American academic-professional sociology on the sociologies of India and Canada have been too obvious to be ignored. Moreover, studying national sociologies in isolation from each other is both misleading and myopic as it conceals the crucial transnational forces that have been so powerful in recent decades.

In our comparative analysis of the sociologies of America, India, and Canada we shall utilize these models to examine the structure and growth of sociology.

Contemporary trends in sociology, it is emphasized (Lazarsfeld, 1973), can only be understood by references to their history. A review of the salient similarities, differences, and unique features of national sociologies could form a basis for a study of the sociology of knowledge. Obviously, this entails an examination of social factors which account for variations and uniformities in national sociologies. Such an inventory could be used as a source of information on data and ideas available in a few countries. Furthermore, such a comparative analysis of national sociologies of the United States of America, India, and Canada should make sociologists aware of problems and procedures they might have overlooked because they were too close to the intellectual trends of their own countries. Moreover, this study, by focusing on the role of American sociology,[6] will tend to show its impact on sociologies in India and Canada, and more importantly, the responses and reactions resulting therefrom. Before we undertake a review of the recent and contemporary trends, it is necessary to explore the basis of sociology within the framework of sociology of knowledge and of sociology. The discussion that follows attempts to identify some of the major issues related to the social milieu and the development of sociological knowledge.

CHAPTER 2

TOWARD A SOCIOLOGY OF SOCIOLOGIES:

Explorations in the Sociology of Knowledge

Sociology, in its present stage of development, is characterized as a "multiple paradigm[1]" science. The discipline of sociology, within a nation and across nations, encompasses a variety of theoretical perspectives, methodologies, and substantive issues. In recent years, there has been a revival of interest in comparative studies, with the ultimate objective of reaching standards of universality in space and time. In this context, the study of sociology in different nations assumes paramount importance.

Divergence in patterns of sociology in different nations have developed with regard to the subject matter of sociology, the methods of research that have been used in the study of society and its problems, and in the explanations that have been offered in response to key theoretical questions. The fundamental question remains as to why the answers have been different not only in different countries but also within a nation.

This crucial issue could be examined in terms of the divergent socio-cultural milieux in which the exponents of the various ideological-theoretical orientations of sociology happen to be, by which they are influenced in their researches and generalizations, and to which they direct their sociological formulations.

Within the sociology of knowledge[2] perspective we can recognize that the growth of sociology as a discipline has, over the years in Europe, North America, and elsewhere, been responding to certain socio-economic forces, as well as to those values cherished by sociologists themselves. It is evident that historical, situational and ideational factors have influenced the nature of sociology within a nation. The production and dissemination of sociological knowledge, its acceptance, rejection, adaptation and unique development in each country is itself a socio-cultural phenomenon.

One of the major tasks confronting the sociology of knowledge is to account for the structure and growth of sociology as an academic discipline. This can be accomplished by an examination of the contributions of individual scholars and through identification of key ideas, schools, theoretical perspectives or paradigms, methodologies, and the processes of institutionalization that are traced across time. It is also relevant to examine the sociology of knowledge in the works of prominent sociologists, their intellectual biases, and their attitudes concerning the relationship between social structures and the production, distribution, and consumption of ideas.

As late as in 1970 it was observed (Curtis and Petras) that there have been no large-scale studies of sociology as a research or teaching enterprise and that no major American or European scholar has yet specialized in research in the sociology of sociology. The paucity of studies and the relative neglect of this area is in itself an interesting sociological problem. It has been emphasized that sociology is not being self critical and sociologists are notorious for studying everything except their own discipline. During the last decade studies of sociology within a sociology of knowledge framework have slowly increased in number. However, there is much that remains to be explored. Several sociologists (Curtis and Petras 1970; Reynolds and Reynolds 1970) have made repeated appeals for more research in the sociology of sociology.

A systematic comparison of theoretical and substantive emphases in contemporary sociology in a number of countries is yet to be undertaken. However, the recent growth of interest in international sociology has contributed a number of descriptive studies of the discipline in several countries (cf. Mohan and Martindale, 1975). Most of these relate the state of the discipline in a particular nation to its unique cultural values and historical developments in social institutions. The comparative evidence from such studies clearly suggests that sociology as it is taught and practiced in a particular society is largely a product of the complex socio-cultural system.

Karl Marx, Karl Mannheim[3] and others have recognized that sociologist's perceptions and thoughts are influenced by the dominant values and social situation which in turn affect research activity and the social construction of reality. These value orientations, either explicit or implicit, cannot be eliminated by refinements in research techniques, but they can be studied and taken into account by others in the interpretation of scientific findings. Furthermore, Robert Lynd, C. Wright Mills, Gunnar Myrdal, Howard Becker, Alvin Gouldner, Friedrichs, among others, have exploded the myth of a value-free sociology. Their main argument seems to suggest that sociology in any country is part of a cultural system and it cannot transcend the dominant values and assumptions of the system.

As sociological research has become empirical, it has become more and more the study of the sociologist's own society. In particular, American sociology has become ethnocentric (Hughes, 1961) in that it has tended to study, in major part, only one society, and has used those methods which are primarily suitable for American society. Consequently, sociological theory developed by American sociologists has been, in major part, parochial and culture-bound.

More importantly, the international expansion of American sociology since World War II has had a considerable impact on the development of other national sociologies. The excessive dependence on American sociology has, on the one hand, tended to create dependency and inhibit the development of theories and models of society appropriate to the social contexts in countries like Canada and India and has prevented the growth of universally valid social theory on the other. Desai (1981) and Sharma (1982) have questioned the relevance and significance of Western - primarily American sociological theories and methods of research to comprehend the social reality of India.

Stolzman and Gamberg (1975) have expressed the view that "the mere accumulation of Canadian data channeled into unexamined American theoretical boxes may bring about an increase in the volume of sociological literature on discrete Canadian topics, but it cannot be the basis for the creation of a genuine Canadian sociology." According to Clark (1975) what has developed in Canada is not a Canadian sociology but a sociology that is American. Lamy (1976) maintains that the dominance of American sociology in Canada has seriously hampered the growth and development of a Canadian sociology with its own communication network, research interest, and ideological commitments, from which might emerge theories and models which differ from those current in American sociology. He further maintains that "one must develop a model that 'fits' one's society, or at least work within a theoretical framework that shows promise of producing one that does."

It is argued that the relationship between cultural and structural dependence tends to be cumulative and interactive; and that excessive cultural dependence on other social science communities is detrimental, in that particular national social science communities may find themselves functioning as 'branch plants' of another social science community. Under these circumstances, sociology may amount to the filling of imported theoretical models with local empirical data. Despite the impact of American sociology on the development of sociology in Canada or India, for example, sociology in these and other countries has not been a replica of the sociology in the United States. From the perspective of the sociology of sociology, perhaps no two national sociologies can be duplicates or photo copies.

However, because of the economic and political dominance of America in world affairs, and the support of university training, research and publications and exchange programs by the federal government and foundations, many scholars from different countries were exposed to American sociology. They tended to accept American social theory, methods and issues with little critical selectiveness or adaptation. The inappropriateness of concepts, theories and illustrations from American sociology and the insensitivity of some foreign sociological research has become a source of conflict and it has in fact stimulated national research.

National sociologies, for reasons obvious, are primarily society and culture-bound. National sociologies attempt to theorize and operationalize research in relation to the experience of specific national societies. The phenomenon of national sociology within a political boundary takes account of historical data, unique features and problems of a society and thereby sociology as a discipline emerges from the society's own view of social reality.

A cursory examination of sociology in different countries reveals that national contexts do influence the questions, problems, and methods the sociologist will choose to investigate social phenomena. The sociological endeavor in each country is affected by dominant ideologies - the national milieu as well as domain assumptions of prominent sociologists.

Furthermore, the relative importance of social issues, government policy, and national needs will influence the way sociology as a discipline is institutionalized, which in turn will shape the nature of sociology in a country. Also, socio-economic and political conditions prompt sociologists to construct and interpret social reality on the basis of their own experiences.

If we link national sociologies with ethnocentric or parochial tendencies of a fragmented[4] discipline, then the quest for sociology as a universal science is enigmatic. National sociologies, as long as they are historically and geographically determined and remain insulated as far as international academic communication is concerned, cannot contribute toward macro level generalizations. However, sociological research within specific national contexts could make a significant contribution to our knowledge about social life in a variety of socio- cultural settings. These cross-national comparative researches, if codified, would facilitate the testing of hypotheses and development of empirically-based and cross-culturally validated theory. Therefore, national sociologies have the potential of reducing ethnocentrism by providing new concepts, theories and paradigms.

From the perspective of the sociology of knowledge, it is argued (Hiller, 1979) that national sociologies are both necessary and inevitable as long as sociological research and theory building takes place in national contexts. Is a universal science of sociology possible? What are the consequences of diverse national sociologies for developing a discipline of sociology that transcends national and/or cultural boundaries? It is believed that a universal science of sociology is possible to the extent that the rules of scientific logic and procedure are globally similar, and that the goal of sociology is to work toward a stronger cross-cultural and cross-national comparative paradigm.

However, to the extent that societies and cultures are too many, ranging from simple to complex social structures, with each society being unique in many respects it is extremely difficult, if not impossible, to explain diverse culture-specific social phenomena with universalistic theory. Therefore, sociology in this respect benefits from national sociologies that try to understand social reality affected by the national milieu through the national traditions, perspectives and cultural ethos.

The sociological research and theory characteristic of each country needs to be frequently reviewed and reinforced, not only through internal debate and rethinking, but also by constant interaction and dialogue with sociologists in other countries to compare research findings and theoretical perspectives. This increased dialogue and comparative analysis of sociological research, theoretical orientations, ideologies, and assumptions, and goals of the sociological endeavor, we would hope, facilitate the growth of a universal science of sociology.

Incidentally, increasing convergence amidst divergence is visible in the sociologies of many countries, so much so that we can discern some significant trends toward a universal sociology. At the moment, however, it is reasonable to assume that these diverse patterns of sociologies of various countries can contribute their share toward the development of global sociology, universal in space and time.

In view of the foregoing debate and controversy in sociology, this study intends to focus on aspects of a central question: What is the role of socio-cultural variables in research and theoretical activity in Sociology? Further to this question, how has sociology in different countries has been shaped by social milieux? What are the similarities and differences in sociology across space and time? What are the transnational forces influencing the growth of sociology in a country?

Utilizing the perspectives of the sociology of knowledge and the sociology of sociology, this research focuses on a cross-national analysis of the discipline of sociology in the

United States, India and Canada. It is an attempt to demonstrate how different national and transnational contexts shape the discipline to produce national sociologies. The major sources of data for this study include several trend reports of sociology and seminal works in social theory and research emanating primarily from these countries. Though the main historical antecedents will be noted, a primary focus will be on the post World War II phenomenon of sociology. Thus, the analyses of the various patterns of sociology in these countries will be diachronic and comparative. This research has implications for the universality of sociology as science in relation to comparative sociology and the contextual relativity of sociological perspectives.

The discussion of a relationship between sociology and social structure demands a synthesis of cross-national comparative data. This would lead the sociology of sociology to a fruitful convergence with the sociology of knowledge in seeking to explore how the problems and conceptions of sociologists are conditioned by the time and the ethos of their societal setting (Tiryakian, 1971).

This study provides an examination of the role sociologists play in their society. Is the sociologist a disinterested or sympathetic observer of society? Does the sociologist see herself/himself as an academic critic, or as an advocate or activist involved in structural change? What are the ethical or moral issues faced by sociologists? What are the dilemmas encountered by sociologists in maintaining objectivity and/or value commitment in their enterprise?

How values and ideals influence the sociological endeavor from the level of 'domain assumptions' sociologists make about certain groups and social phenomena, categories or variables, to the level of how and what facts are collected and how they are interpreted or explained? The role of values and ideology in sociological research and theory raises questions such as: Why and how do the values expressed or implied in some sociological theory or method become accepted over others, and under what conditions do they go out of favor? What social factors account for some sociological group or school in a country achieving intellectual dominance over contrasting groups or schools? What accounts for vogues in fields which tempt the research interests of sociologists or vogues in financial support for certain kinds of sociological research? An analysis of the process of institutionalization of sociology in different countries is also important. What are the major differentials in the socialization and recruiting process of sociologists? What kinds of formal and informal structures and social networks interrelate different groups in the profession? Equally significant are some fundamental questions such as: Sociology by whom?; for whom?; and most importantly, for what ends? This study attempts to examine some of these major questions.

American sociology has attained a preeminent position in world sociology. Its hegemonic influence over several national sociologies makes it necessary to discuss the social context in which American sociology has developed. The discussion that follows sketches its evolutionary patterns, contemporary trends and issues, and its influence on the sociologies of India and Canada.

CHAPTER 3

PARADIGMS AND HEGEMONY:

American Sociology

"To much of the world today, sociology is practically synonymous with American sociology. The preeminence of American sociology in its professional sphere throughout the world may be even greater than the corresponding world influence of most other American cultural efforts. Its techniques are everywhere emulated, and its theories shape the terms in which world discussion of sociology is cast and the issues around which intellectual debate centers.

American sociology today is, for all practical purposes, the model of academic sociology throughout the world....Since intellectual tendencies do not develop in a social vacuum, any effort to understand American sociology today must relate it to the nature and problems of the society in which it developed."
                                                            -Gouldner.

In the context of the comments made by Gouldner, the discussion that follows is intended to demonstrate the influence of social forces on the development of American sociology and its hegemony in much of the world today.

American sociology is characterized by its internal diversity in terms of theoretical perspectives, methodologies, and growing subspecialties; and by its external hegemony, especially since World War II. It is not our intention to provide a comprehensive history and critique of American sociology. That would constitute a separate volume and, there are many works (Hinkle, 1980; Bierstedt, 1981; Merton, 1959; Parsons, 1968; Short, 1981) that have already accomplished this task. Here we would like to briefly outline some of the important evolutionary patterns and salient recent and contemporary trends and issues in American sociology that tend to have relevance for an understanding of its influence on the sociologies of India and Canada.

The role of changing American culture and social structure in the development of modern American sociology has been noted by several sociologists (Wolff, 1946; Page, 1954; Hinkle and Hinkle, 1954; Tiryakian, 1971; Reynolds and Reynolds, 1970; Friederichs, 1970; Curtis and Petras, 1970; Gouldner 1970). Sociology in the United States developed as an intellectual offshoot of Western social thought under the influence of early European sociologists such as Comte, Spencer, Marx, Durkheim, Weber, Simmel, and several others, in the last half of the nineteenth century. Although American sociology is a product of both European and American intellectual influences, the discipline is considered to be uniquely American[1] in organization and development.

In the early decades of its growth, American sociology was characterized by an emphasis on theories of social change. In addition, a deductive approach had developed into an interest in social structure and the forms and processes of society. Sociological studies were viewed as primarily focusing on the relation between the individual and society or various aspects of the larger whole, involving the psychological, physical, and socio-cultural aspects of society. Particular schools of thought and scholars associated with this early trend in American sociology are community and ecological studies (Park and Burgess), structural-functional analysis (Sumner, Giddings, Cooley), and the study of psychological forms (Ross, Thomas, Mead) in social interaction (Zimmerman 1958: 3-8).

Beginning in 1920, American sociology became predominantly characterized by a trend which has been termed neo-positivistic empiricism. Sociological neo-positivism has its roots in the quantitative approach which emphasizes enumeration and measurement; behaviourism which dictates that social science should confine itself to the study of observable behaviour; and pragmatism. (Valien and Valien, 1957:86) This school of sociological thought has attempted sociological investigations based on the collection of "facts" or has assumed an inductive method of inquiry. The quantification aspect of neo-positivistic sociology has meant a type of natural science approach for sociology making it more of an "exact science". This kind of American empiricism gained headway in other countries due to American influence. (Zimmerman, 1958: 10-11).

Social statics as the major focus for study has not been completely abandoned. On the contrary this approach to sociology has evolved into social action theory. The major figures in the development of social action theory have been identified as T. Znaniecki, R.M. MacIver, H. Becker, E. Shils and T. Parsons, the latter three acknowledging the influence of Max Weber in their work (Valien and Valien, 1957: 87). The social action theory approach contains a number of elements contradictory to neo-positivism. Social action theorists propose that social science does not necessarily have to confine itself to studying observable behaviour; that is, introspection can be a valuable source of scientific data regarding human behaviour. They also oppose the indiscriminate use of quantitative methods and the application of behaviourist, reductionist psychology to sociology.

The trends toward more marcoscopic analysis and the questioning of the use of case studies are in contrast to previous attitudes of American sociologists in these areas. American sociology has traditionally been less concerned with macroscopic interpretation and has put more emphasis on social problems. While European sociologists have been interested in broad theories and philosophies of societal development, Americans usually took for granted the general outline of society and its major values. The applied interests of early American sociologists seem to stem from an identification of sociology with religiously defined ethical duties and with philanthropy, both of which became institutionalized in aspects of community service and social work. Many early American sociologists had been trained as ministers, and often departments of sociology and social work were combined in universities. (Parsons, 1959)

II

Since the end of World War II, it appears that neo-positivistic empiricism has continued to dominate American sociology. This trend has developed along with, and has been aided by, the increasing availability of computer facilities and the growth of statistical and mathematical research tools and methods. Bogardus (1973: 145-151) has commented that in 1972 few American sociological laboratories of any size were without computers or access to them. The use of computers coupled with empiricism have given quantitative sociology a boost, and new techniques for analyzing social phenomena are continually being developed. The increased ability to handle large amounts of data has not yielded complete pictures of the problems studied. Accompanying the use in macro-level studies has been increasing criticism of the use of case studies. Using case studies has retained a place in sociological inquiry, but it is now recognized that the cases chosen must be representative. If they are not, then investigation must make clear how cases are unique.

American sociology has also seen increasing specialization and diversification. The growth of sociological specialities has often been organized in terms of research "centres" focusing on particular aspect of social life such as family, population, crime, aging or youth problems. There has been much diversity in social theories, with various sociologists advancing for example behaviorism, social field theory, humanistic theories, general theory of deviant behaviour and social theories of race relations. With the increasing specialization and diversification, some basic problems have been created, in that the central core of sociology may be seriously weakened. Diversity and specialization can only be of their greatest value to the progress of sociology if they are carried out with some consideration of their relationship to sociology as a whole.

During the 1960s and early 1970s there was a marked shift of some sociology professors from teaching to research activities. At least, many have had their teaching duties substantially reduced so that they are free to engage in part-time research or to serve in government and other public committees and commissions. The increased research activities of a significant number of sociologists has had some detrimental side effects on the teaching of sociology in American universities. This research vitality of American sociology has also been related to the great expansion in publication channels and distribution of sociological journals in the United States. Many new sociological journals have begun publication as older ones have increased in size and quality and become functionally differentiated. During the 1950-1970 period several new subspecialties emerged and traditional specialities expanded in terms of teaching and research output (Stehr and Larson, 1972).

One of the problems in American sociology appears to be the unclarified relationship between social psychology and sociology. The psychologist has maintained a strong psychological interpretation and the sociologist has insisted on sociological approach to the understanding of social psychological phenomenon. (Bogardus, 1973) The fact that these differences have not been resolved is surprising because American sociology has emphasized social psychology. Two studies of areas of specialization in American sociology found that social psychology ranked first for a period of approximately twenty five years (Brown and Gilmartin, 1969; 284; Stehr and Larson, 1972: 5).

Despite the theoretical diversity, the increased use of computers and mathematical tools and greater numbers of macro level studies mentioned earlier, American sociology has still remained very empirical, and theoretical development has been weak. It has been suggested that Americans need to spend time in the systematic formulation of coherent sets of empirical generalizations into theory. For this theoretical development to take place, the general scope of much research will have to be altered. Brown and Gilmartin (1969: 288-290) found that research published in two prestigious American journals was very culture and time-bound. Three quarters of the research was found to have its setting in the United States and eighty-five percent referred to only one point in time, usually the present. Before American sociology can reach some level of theoretical development, it will have to transcend American national culture and put some emphasis on cross-cultural national and historical research.[2] (cf. Marsh, Hughes, Webber, Hollander). We will return to this theme of ethnocentrism in American   sociology later in our discussion.

With this background of the antecedents, growth, and general trends, let us turn our attention to the major theoretical schools

- perspectives that have been exerting influence in American sociology during the past three decades (1950-1980).

III

For Gouldner, to understand the character of academic sociology we have to understand the domain assumptions of theories. He believed that all social theory is immersed in a sub-theoretical level of domain assumptions and sentiments which both liberate and constrain it. In fact, all theory is not merely influenced by a group but actually produced by a group. In other words, sociology necessarily operates within the limits of its assumptions, and sociologists tend to organize their researches in terms of their prior assumptions about people and society.

Furthermore, Gouldner maintained that 'theory is the head of the hammer; background assumptions are the handle on which the hammer's head rests, without which it could not be wielded but of which we have only tacit awareness.' Writing about the events of the 1960s and their influence on sociology, Gouldner observed that 'social theorists today work within a crumbling social matrix of paralysed urban centers and battered campuses...We theorize today within the sound of guns.' It is in this context of domain assumptions of theories and environmental forces that the encounter of traditional and emerging paradigms in sociology can be examined.

Several organizational and classificatory structures have been used in the description and analysis of social theory. Various books on social theory have been organized either on the basis of core concepts (Nisbet, 1966) or on biographies of individual thinkers (Bierstadt, 1981; Barnes, 1948; Coser, 1971) in chronological order (Zeitlin, 1968). Others (Turner, 1982; Poloma, 1979; Skidmore, 1975; Wallace, 1980 Ritzer) have discussed social theory based either on intellectual history which analyzes interrelations among the works of several authors who are assumed to have influenced one another, or on schools of social thought. Using the same or different organizational structure, sociologists, in recent years, have attempted to present a wide variety[3] of complex schemes for categorizing social theories - schools - paradigms - perspectives ranging from structural-functional, conflict, symbolic interaction, exchange to that of ethnomethodology, critical theory, and social biology.

From the standpoint of the sociology of knowledge, Mullins (1973) presents a four-stage theoretical model for the development of theories marked by empirically demonstrable social and intellectual characteristics. The four stages of the growth of theories are: (i) normal, (ii) network; (iii) cluster; (iv) specialty or discipline. In this process of theory development the emphasis is more on communication, coauthorship, apprenticeship and colleagueship characteristic of sociologists.

For Martindale (1979) it is necessary to distinguish between ideologies and scientific theories, because ideologies possess persuasive intent and orient themselves toward what the world ought to be like. Theories, however, are simple descriptions and explanations of some phenomenon - what is. He rejects the term 'paradigm' because of its ambiguous meaning and believes that very little is gained by explicating sociology as a science populated by multiple paradigms. Martindale's classification system based on the methodological choice of positivism or non-positivism classifies the types of theories according to their elementaristic or holistic character.

On the other hand, Ritzer (1975) thinks that sociology consists of multiple paradigms even though there may be disagreement about the quantity and nature of them. According to him, sociology is dominated by three paradigms: social factism, social definitionism, and social behaviourism. Each paradigm emphasizes only selected aspects of behavior: macro-objective, macro-subjective, micro-objective, micro-subjective. So he argues (1979) that sociology needs an integrated paradigm which can synthesize these four basic levels of social reality. Ritzer makes a strong case for the idea that an integrated paradigm must be comparative, historical, and dialectical. Furthermore, sociology must never be content with individual ramifications or group ideologies, but must look instead for the 'real' nature of social reality. In this context, it should be noted that the term 'paradigm' in sociological literature is being used interchangeably with terms such as 'orientation', 'theory', 'model', 'perspective'. (cf. Turner, 1982: 14; Lee, 1982: 85-101; Merton, 1968: 69ff; 104ff). Harvey (1982: 85-101) shows how sociologists have used the term 'paradigm' in a loose and inconsistent fashion in order to classify aspects of sociological knowledge, and how as a result the utility of the concept, that derives, in each case, from Kuhn's initial formulation has been lost.

The term 'paradigm' has been used (Ritzer) to mean exemplar, methodological style, theory, theroetical orientation, ideology, philosophical perspective and various combinations of these. According to Masterman, in his book 'Structure of Scientific Revolutions' Kuhn used the term in twenty-one different ways.

Harvey points out that Kuhn's conceptualization of paradigmatic development in science is not easily amenable to incorporation in to the social sciences without considerable adaptation. The usage of 'paradigm' in sociological literature fails to take account of the process of change or paradigmatic shift in the social sciences. It is noted that those sociologists who talk of the multi-paradigmatic state of sociology are usually the worst offenders for ignoring the processual aspect of paradigmatic analysis. Furthermore, it is argued that Kuhn's usage of the term paradigm and the usage in sociology are not the same. Within the sociology of knowledge, the term similarly ignores the essential features of Kuhnian paradigms; that they should be successive, monopolistic, and incompatible. Whether, in the case of sociology, the conclusion is that the discipline is pre-paradigmatic or that a succession of overlapping paradigms are in evidence, is a matter for further research.

During the last few years, sociology has been involved in self reflection and self-evaluation. The diversity of approaches and theoretical frameworks evident in contemporary sociological analysis leads us to conclude that sociology is composed of multiple paradigms. Metasociology, i.e. the effort to find the underlying bases of sociology, has not only tried to identify the characteristics of prevailing paradigms but has also taken steps toward the development of new sociological paradigms.

According to Kuhn, it is not cumulation of knowledge that contributes to the truly major changes in science, but revolution. At any given point in time a science is dominated by a specific paradigm. As anomalies increase which can't be explained by the dominant paradigm a crisis occurs leading to a scientific revolution and the emergence of new dominant paradigm.

Just as a paradigm serves to differentiate one scientific community from another (Ritzer 1981: 3) paradigms can also be used to differentiate among subcommunities within the same science. It is in this sense that there are multiple paradigms in sociology.

It is true that sociology has rarely been dominated by one theory; yet some have achieved relative hegemony during certain periods of its growth. Sociology has experienced (Wiley, 1979) four distinct phases each mainfesting the dominance of a theoretical orientation with the exception of the contemporary phase: the evolutionary, the Chicago school, functionalism, and the contemporary interregnum. By the mid 1970s both theory and methods were inundated with variations of older themes: dialects, ideal types, ethnomethodology, and phenomenology.

Tiryakian (1979) asserts that the dominance of certain schools of thought is dependent upon a founder-leader, disciplines, social organization and publication channels. Based on these variables, he discusses the emergence and dominance of three major schools of sociology: the Durkeimian school, the Chicago school, and the Parsonian school. Each of these frameworks has its merits and limitations.

Having noted these different organizational structures and categories of description and analysis of social theories, let us examine briefly some of the influential theoretical schools: structural- functional, conflict, symbolic interaction, exchange, ethnomethodology, phenomenology, critical and radical sociology, and socio-biology. It is extremely difficult to separate ideologies from sociological theories, as ideologies seem to be either explicitly or implicity part of most theories. Recognizing this fact we wish to show the biases and value assumptions associated with each of these theoretical schools.

In contemporary American sociology, the adherents of different theoretical schools are largely aware of one another. While often talking past one another, they do address some key theoretical questions such as the nature of social order and social change at macro and micro levels of social reality. Moreover, most of these schools and the controversies among them are to some degree oriented to common areas of research. Yet very often it is difficult to find in these discussions any degree of consensus. "Instead these schools often evince", as Eisenstadt (1981: 329) states, "strong, sectarian, and ideological tendencies which keep each of them in a closed niche, making proclamations about the superiority of each against all the others".

The structural-functional school has been a major analytical perspective in sociology. It has contributed to an understanding of the relations between personalities, social systems, and culture by relating itself to many of the important developments in anthropology, psychology, organizational and systems theory. It has provided insights into the major mechanisms through which individual and organizational behavior contributes to the functioning of societies as social systems.

The relative predominance of the structural-functional school is attributed to its close relation to the classical problem of sociology; its elaboration of a new systematic, conceptual and analytical apparatus for analysis of societal relations, behavior, and organizations; and its generation of research programs that are claimed to be objective-scientific and of far reaching theoretical significance. But it is quite evident that the structural-functional school has addressed itself to the problem of how the dimension of solidarity-integration-equilibrium, meaning and trust are institutionalized in the construction and maintenance of social order.

This model is criticized as ahistorical, tautological, and teleological. The underlying assumption of the structural-functional school is to the effect that social order is based upon central social values and value integration, which bring about social consensus. It emphasizes the boundary maintaining mechanisms of social control and minimizes or rather neglects the importance of power and coercion as means of social integration. This model, by exaggerating the unity, stability, and harmony of social systems tends to perserve the **status quo**. It does not adequately reflect phenomena like power, conflict, deviance and change. Therefore, the structural functional school of sociology has, obviously, tended to be a social theory that happens to be conservative in its underlying assumptions and values.

It has often been claimed that the structural-functional perspective is better able to account for the persistent features of societies and that conflict theory is better able to account for changes in societies. The ideological thrust of these schools is evident in the fact that conflict theorists give greater emphasis to conflict, dysfunction, and social change because they are personally more likely to desire radical change. Whereas structural-functional theorists tend to give more attention to functions, cooperation, stability, **status quo** because they are personally less likely to desire radical change and more likely to prefer some reform of present social arrangements. Structural functionalism asks how society is able to function; conflict theory asks why some groups benefit from the social order more than others. Although some efforts have been made to synthesize these two theories many unresolved issues (Adams 1966) still remain.

'Mainstream' sociology (i.e. structural-functional school) is accused of being positivistic; and its methods are considered to be closely related to a technocratic orientation and perception of society. By accepting the status quo, main-stream sociology is said to be devoid of the critical dimension in sociological analysis. This conservative theoretical approach necessitated a more reflective, critical, and ideologically committed social theory.

The conflict theory (especially of the Marxist and Neo-Marxist traditions), however, tends to make excessive claims as to the dominant role of conflict in all social relationships and in all social systems, instead of viewing conflict as one of many processes in society. Conflict theory as theory, and not polemics, does provide a valuable theoretical perspective in understanding patterns of continuity and change among different types of social units. The classical and contemporary Marxist approaches have stressed the relation between the power elements and characteristics of structure and dynamics of social systems with special emphasis on conflicts and contradictions of such systems. The neo-Marxist approaches have made major contributions to the study of traditional and modern societies. These studies are in contrast to those using the structural functional approach in that neo-Marxist conflict approach is historical, macro-societal, comparative and dialectical.

Neo-Marxist sociologists have labeled mainstream sociology as 'corporate sociology', 'bourgeois sociology', 'establishment sociology' because the structural functional or systems analysis is considered to be contributing to the main tenets of corporate capitalism. Szymanski (1971) demonstrates that the basic orientations, concepts, problems, and theories of American sociology are determined, at least in broad outline, by the corporate system of which it is a part and it fulfills the system's needs for legitimation of social reality that explains and justifies the existing social order and its dominant interests. Abstracted empiricism and grand theory (Parsonian) are considered to be adequate enough as legitimating mechanisms by the establishment; and for manipulation and control.

It is believed that the social structure of sociology is determined by the dominant institutional structure of the society in which sociology is a part. Universities, the sociology department, research institutions as bureaucracies where sociological activities take place are closely tied to the interests of corporations and government. An overwhelming majority of sociologists working in bureaucratic institutions cannot be value-free, especially in the analysis of data and problems, as far as research projects supported by corporations and government agencies are concerned.

The major mechanisms that reinforce the consensus among the subscribers to a 'hegemonic mode of sociology' are: the reading of the same journals, and attendance at the same conferences; the demands of one's clients and superiors to conform; the informal association with one's colleagues; the necessity to adhere to the rules of the game in order to achieve rewards from the system. Furthermore, the dominant groups within sociology control the sociology department structure, the socialization of the next generation by teaching their kind of sociology, jobs, research grants, journals, offices of professional organizations etc.

Sociology, by and large, has been subservient to the needs for practical knowledge and legitimation of the corporate system. The corporate system in its efforts to achieve these ends rewards those sociologists who help to maintain the dominant values and definitions of social reality. So, it is argued that the content of contemporary mainstream sociology is determined by the functions of sociology for the dominant system of order.

As an alternative to the bureaucratized orientation of mainstream sociology, Szymanski (1971) advocated a 'radical sociology' based on a different set of orientations, i.e. (i) a driving and relentless curiosity to understand society; (ii) a deep and healthy criticism toward all received and established ideas, both within and outside of sociology; (iii) a fundamental compassion for people, and an identification with the victims of the routine workings of social structures. A radical sociology looks for explanations of social life and theories of society which assume that radical change is at least possible, and resists those theories which root inequality in "inescapable facts" of biology or social structure (Becker and Horowitz 1972: 53).

The radical sociologist is expected to serve as a constant social critic of the dominant institutional structures and relate people's problems and day-to-day concerns to the dynamics of social structures, thereby translating them into political issues. Radical sociologists should feel a basic identity with the victims of oppressive social structures.

In other words, radical sociology must elaborate a counter definition of social reality. The goal of radical sociology is, above all, the formulation and propagation of a sociology relevant to the practical problems facing humanity. Radical sociology is supposed to contribute to the building of a 'decent' and humane society through an understanding of its structure and dynamics and through the dissemination of these understandings to the public. In this sense, radical sociology aims to be critical, humanistic, reflexive, value-committed, issue and change oriented applied sociology.

It appears that this kind of radical sociology emerged as a response to a number of events and processes of the 1960s. The civil rights movement, race riots, the feminist movement, the Vietnam war, War on Poverty, economic, political and military strength of the United States giving rise to inequality and injustice at home and its foreign policy affecting youth and protest movements on university campuses - all these anti-establishment activities seem to have contributed to spark a revolt against what is called the 'establishment sociology'. It is in this context, Gouldner (1970) noted, that social theorists work within a crumbling social matrix of paralyzed urban centers and battered campuses and theorize within the sound of guns.

As systems theory found it difficult to fully explain the events of the 1960's, conflict theory began to gain ground in academic sociology. It is observed (Frumkin, 1975: 135) that the resistance of the systems theorists to the change theorists in the 1950s and the lack of consensus among American sociological theorists in the 1960s reflect the early stages of the scientific revolution in sociology suggested by Kuhn (1970).

IV
Besides these two dominant schools (structural-functional and conflict), there have been a few micro-sociological theories-schools- perspectives such as symbolic interactionism, exchange theory, and ethnomethodology focusing on face-to-face, interpersonal or small group level of human interaction. Compared to the dominant schools, these micro approaches, though having limited numbers of followers, have demonstrated their significance

in sociological analysis by stretching and applying these theories to explain large scale social units as well.

The symbolic interactionist (Blumer, 1969) perspective looks at human interactions by analyzing the use of shared symbols, such as language, values, definitions as the basis for social organization. The manner in which an individual's personal interpretations of the world, his/her subjective reality, are shaped and affected by interaction is emphasized by those sociologists who follow this school.

Symbolic interactionists believe that the study of two or a few people interacting can tell them a great deal about what the values and expectations of the whole society are. This school represents a strong humanistic position against the neopositivistic emphasis in sociological theory. Critics of the interactionist perspective object that it is too narrow in scope; it does not pay enough attention to the importance of social institutions or to the powerful forces of change acting through power, authority, inequality, class struggle and conflict.

Exchange theory has been useful in explaining face-to-face relations and behaviour in small group situations. The advocates of this brand of exchange theory (Homans, 1974) believe that the goal of human behaviour is to maximize pleasure, profits or rewards and minimize or avoid pain, loss or punishment and that all social phenomena may be analyzed in terms of exchange. It is pointed out that exchange theory does not deal with the complexity of human behaviour, that it fails to deal adequately with systemic needs, and that, by following a rather narrow behaviourist approach, it suffers from psychological reductionism.

Efforts are made (Blau, 1976) to extend exchange theory to analyze the workings of institutions and larger complex structures. This micro-macro level approach of exchange theory recognizes power, stratification, exploitation, the dialectical process and change of collectivities. However, the underlying assumption that much human behaviour is based upon exchange remains the same for the adherents of this theoretical perspective.

Ethnomethodology (Garfinkel, 1967) observes the methods used by individuals in constructing social reality as the first step in constructing sociological knowledge. Ethnomethodology shares with exchange and symbolic interation the notion that the individual is the main actor. Like symbolic interactionism, ethnomethodology is a social psychological approach concerned with individuals rather than social structures, but the questions raised are different from those of symbolic interactionism. Ethnomethodology does not accept the functionlists' assumption that social facts have a reality of their own that impinge on the individual.

Phenomenology, likewise, challenges the naturalistic-positivistic assumptions and stresses the primacy of consciousness and subjective meaning in the interpretation of social action. It is concerned with how the subjective states of actors are created, maintained, or changed. Phenomenologists seem to differ in their recognition of an external social world and regarding assumptions about an external world. While criticising alternate forms of theorizing, phenomenologists assert the primacy of studying the processes of human consciousness.

Structuralism (Levi-Strauss, 1967) goes beyond emphasis on the symbolic dimension in the construction of culture and society and claims that there exists within any culture some 'hidden structure' which is more important than that which appears overtly in social organization. In contrast, the Marxists have emphasized both power and symbolic dimensions - the dialectic between forces and relations of production, class consciousness, alienation, class struggle - as processes that provide principles of the deep structure of societies explaining their complex institutional characteristics and dynamics.

The biological school seemed to have been revitalized in the mid 1970's. Sociobiology, (Wilson, 1975) incorporating various aspects of evolutionary biology and the social sciences provides a counter perspective in sociology. It claims that certain elements of human behavior are best understood in terms of biological predispositions. This approach has been severely criticized as racist and/or sexist, since biological explanations preclude the possibility of change in human behavior through environmental influences. This perspective, with a very limited number of adherents, has generated a heated ideological debate.

These different theoretical orientations not only ask different questions, but frequently come up with different answers. None is necessarily absolutely right nor wrong in explaining social reality or in comprehending truth in its totality. They tend to be partial theories. It seems that societies are so complex that they cannot be fully understood through one theoretical orientation or model. The development of sociological knowledge obviously rests on the contributions of different orientations-perspectives-paradigms.

Kinloch (1981) has delineated significant variations in the ideological elements involved in contemporary sociological theory and identifies three types of ideologies: conservative, radical and liberal as the underlying basis of most contemporary theories and demonstrates how these ideological biases of theories influence perception of problems, their causes, consequences, and the prescriptions for solution of problems.

He observes that 'mainstream' American sociology represents an attempt by the bourgeoisie to impose rationality on contemporary industrial society. Its concern with thinkers who critique the foundation of contemporary society and awareness of personal ideology of sociologists are limited.

Furthermore, he argues that "until and unless the discipline broadens its social, philosophical, and ideological base, it will remain naive and impractical as the speech mode of middle class establishment academia. For sociology to be relevant to the needs of modern society, it must reflect the characteristics of the social structure as a whole rather than only that of rational, middle class, professional social scientists. Involvement of the perspectives and activities of all social groups, minorities in particular, is required if such relevance is to be achieved. Otherwise, the discipline will continue to address only itself and its establishment supporters. Sociology will continue as ideology - the science of its own position in society rather than of social problems in general. Concern with the societal effects of particular definitions of reality and factors behind the belief in rationality may at least represent limited moves in a more relevant direction.

According to Kinloch, 'while it is clearly impossible to totally overcome inevitable ideological boundaries, the attempt to expand the theoretical concern beyond subgroup interests to society as a whole reduces in practical policy terms at least the narrowness of such egocentric concerns'...'This calls for a rather different kind of sociology than the present in existence, nevertheless, if the discipline and profession are ever to become more than ideology, such concerns must be addressed. Otherwise sociology will continue to represent the conservative theoretical reaction of establishment thinkers to the issues posed by social change - the speech mode of the privileged, which elaborates the status quo and makes it scientifically respectable at the 'taxpayer's expense'.

Merton (1975:28) a structural functionalist believes that "the chronic crisis of sociology, with its diversity, competition and clash of doctrine, seems preferable to the therapy sometimes proposed for handling the acute crisis, namely, the prescription of a single theoretical perspective that promises to provide full and exclusive access to sociological truth."

All these variety of theoretical perspectives do in fact demonstrate a process of widening the framework of sociological analysis and the examination of key issues of social structure and change. The prevalence of different theoretical models provides the possibility of enriching sociological research. However, because of sectarian tendencies, controversies, and relative insulation among different schools and its adherents, cross fertilization, synthesis or use of multiple approaches among sociologists have rarely begun to be accomplished.

The underlying problem seems to be in the fact that most of these controversies have been intertwined with socio-economic, political events, processes and ideological trends such as the Civil Rights, Feminist and Youth movements, student protest, Vietnam War, Water Gate, poverty, inflation, unemployment, injustice, consumer and environmental issues that surfaced during the 1960s and 1970s.

Closely related has been the shift to growing preoccupation with meta theory and meta scientific problems such as the epistomological, philosophical and ideological foundations of sociological theory, method and research. This has been reflected in the works of Gouldner (1970), Friedrichs (1970), and Snizek (1979), among others. However, the parochialism within sociology, characterized by the use of different approaches when dealing with similar problems and lack of interaction among those having different orientations appears to be a major hurdle in the development and acceptance of an integrated paradigm.

Various political events and social processes of the post World War II era, especially of the 1960s and 1970s, seem to have influenced the emergence of new branches of sociology based on different intellectual orientations and social issues. Existential sociology, Cognitive sociology, Humanist sociology, Environmental sociology, Black sociology, Feminist sociology are a few among many sociologies that have proliferated during the last few years. Sociology appears to have reached an impasse because of this critical fragmentation of the sociological community into several splintered groups each having their own orientations and goals. This is not to say that there is no overlap among these new sociologies. However, this increasing balkanization within sociology has contributed to a greater degree of sectarianism and loss of mutual contacts among different approaches even when sociologists deal with similar problems.

The frequent controversies and disagreements within sociology over theoretical perspectives and research methods seem to be resulting from increasing fragmentation and diversification of sociology along theoretical and substantive areas on the one hand and insulation among sociologists of different interests and persuasions on the other. The increasing specialization, and the massive amounts of published literature make it extremely difficult for sociologists to keep abreast of recent developments in research and theory even in a specialized branch of sociology, let alone the entire field of sociology.[4]

Many contemporary sociologists interested in specific branches of sociology tend to read, indulge in research, and publish, in very specialized areas. Sociologists appear to build their career around such specialties. As a result of numerous specialized branches of sociology which have resulted, it is rather difficult to conceive of sociology as a single discipline with a single paradigm. In fact, some sociologists think that sociology is still in a pre-paradigmatic stage, while others assert that sociology possesses multiple paradigms, and still others claim that sociology is facing a crisis of paradigms. This state of affairs of sociology gives the impression that it is now a discipline in name only, though most sociologists tend to work in college and university departments of sociology, and adhere to national and international professional organizations and conferences. As Becker (1979) puts it, "it is not one world in sociology any more. Rather, what we have is a loosely connected network of specialty subworlds, which operate and work together mostly at the departmental level. All the subspecialties subscribe to a common ancestor (Durkheim, Marx-Weber) myth, in whose name they look for the links that bind together their in fact quite different areas of work."

The proliferation of subspecialties aside, the large number and variety of competing theories in sociology is considered (Zelditch, 1979) to be a sign of vitality. It is also stated (Rabow and Zucker, 1980) that the efforts by sociologists to deny the validity of alternative perspectives does little to contribute to the advancement of knowledge. The factionalism and the controversies among different sociological schools (for eg: structural functional/conflict; symbolic interaction/ethno-methodology) over specification and methods of study tend to assert that one's theory-method-paradigm is 'superior' and 'right' and all the others are not.

Some sociologists seem to think that there is an ultimate singular truth about society which can be reached by following the best paradigm, which they alone claim to possess. At the present stage of apparent crisis and chaos, it is maintained by others (Merton, 1975; Zelditch, 1979), however, that sociology benefits most from encouraging diversity and richness of theories-paradigms and least from prematurely rejecting novel and innovative paradigms.

Kuhn suggests that there are a number of non-objective factors involved in the adoption of a paradigm or a view of the world. Therefore, to comprehend social reality as completely as possible it is necessary to encourage alternative theories, paradigms, perspectives in sociology. Given the fact that there are multiple truths about society, sociology has to accept the value and the need for diverse perspectives- theories-paradigms.[5] As a consequence, it is hoped that the core of sociological knowledge would increase and isolation of specialties, approaches or paradigms would decrease.

Apart from the multiplicity of theoretical perspectives, there has been greater emphasis on research methodology, especially by neopositivists. Most sociologists tend to equate science and method, and see methodological refinement as more appropriate than theoretical debate in American sociology. It is argued (Gray, 1979: 35-42) that methodology, no matter how sophisticated is no substitute for conceptualization. The common qualities of essential sociology are considered to be: (a) the subject investigated is important to human beings; (b) the investigation proceeds analytically, with all the methodological sophistication available, and with scholarly regard for facts; (c) the analysis should be based on historically grounded theory and research. There seems to be a consensus as to the need for subordination of method to substance because of the belief that no amount of methodological brilliance will compensate for theoretical weakness. (Coser, 1975: 692).

Domain assumptions, according to Gouldner (1970: 49-56) are built not only into substantive social theory but into methodology itself. Research methods, asserts Gouldner, always premise the existence and use of some system of social control since human beings are considered as 'things' or 'subjects' who may be treated and controlled or manipulated in much the same manner that other sciences control their non-human materials. To the extent that sociology follows the physical science model,[6] there is a repressive technocratic current in research methodology.

We are indeed living in an age of 'testomania and testocracy', as Sorokin (1956) observed. Quantophrenia and testomania have spread like epidemics in the Western countries where almost every individual is tested from the cradle to the grave. He showed that the 'scientific' tests and the results of tests are not free from subjective estimates and arbitrary interpretations. Sociology has no doubt moved from description to the development of more or less precise increasingly complex quantitative models. However, these mathematical models are bound by time and culture and have remained ideographic rather than nomothetic. Despite these limitations, American research methods and techniques are emulated in India and in Canada (a theme that will be examined in subsequent chapters), and in many other countries. A review of recent work on quantitative methods (Schuessler, 1980: 835-860) suggests that it consists of largely of adapting methods developed elsewhere in statistics, demography, economics, engineering - for answering relatively simple questions about social change (or permanence) that reflect practical concerns no less than theoretical ones.

For Coser (1975: 691-700) the serious problems faced by the discipline have been created, or at least accentuated, by the resolution in methodology and research technology. The modern techniques of regression and path analysis, he believes, are leading to a situation where the methodological tail wags the substantive dog. The fallacy of misplaced precision i.e. the belief that one can compensate for theoretical weakness by methodological strength has a tendency to produce young sociologists with superior research skills but with a trained incapacity to think in theoretically innovative ways. Coser argues that the prevailing American ideology of individual achievement combined with the use of statistical methods in limited areas, prevents the growth of sociology and curtails sociologists' ability to strive for a full accounting and explanation of the major societal forces. This 'hypertrophy of method at the expense of substantive theory' in American sociology seems to foster the growth of both 'narrow, routine activities, and of sect-like, esoteric ruminations - an expression of crisis and fatigue within the discipline and its theoretical underpinnings!.

During the 1950s and 1960s there was an emphasis on 'methodology' - the 'hard', 'quantitative', systematic empiricism as a major means of arriving at truth. Positivism's hegemonic rise was attributed (Antonio and Piran, 1978) to the depoliticization of social science for the protection of elites who utilize science for domination, the rise of mass society and bureaucratic domination, and the lack of organic community mediated by strong familiar and communal bonds. The emphasis on positivism - ahistorical, particularist analysis - it is claimed, has not resulted in the emergence of a coherent image of the social reality. Instead, as research findings accumulate the image of the social world becomes increasingly confused, complex, fragmented and qualified. This has occured because most American sociologists generally lack comparative epistemologies and indulge in trivial and chaotic empirical data. Therefore, as an alternative to positivism, it is asserted that Marx's epistemology and his method of immanent critique - empirical analysis of historically relevant contemporary issues and events - should be used in a critical, self-conscious manner.

Furthermore, it is contended (Wardell and Fuhrman, 1981) that sociology occupies an alienated position within capitalist society where positivist epistemology serves as an ideological veil, concealing the existence of ontological presuppositions, distorting social reality, and preventing any meaningful attempt to understand the dynamics of society. It is argued that the dominance of positivism within sociology, moreover, gives it a hegemonic status, negating any recognition that the individual and society are interdependent. It is in this sense perhaps the outstandingly persistent feature of American sociology is said to be its 'voluntaristic nominalism', (Hinkle and Hinkle, 1954). Some American sociologists (cf. Rossi, 1980) think that if American sociology has made greater headway in influencing social policy, it is largely because of methodological competence rather than conceptual perspectives.

VI
There have been studies identifying ideological-class bias in various substantive areas. Ideological currents and class bias have been recognized in American sociological research in the fields of stratification (Pease, 1970; Hofley, 1971), family (Stolte Heiskanen, 1971; Burr et al, 1979) law, crime and deviance (Greenaway, 1900; Schervish, 1973; Thio 1973), political process (Moskos, 1967), social problems (Horton, 1966; Becker, 1967), race (Myrdal, 1944; Rex, 1977; Stone, 1977) urban sociology (Castells 1976). Becker and Horowitz (1972: 48-66) have stressed the fact that sociological research by and large, is designed to further the interests of the powerful at the expense of the powerless.[7] For instance, prison research has for the most part been oriented to problems of jailers rather than those of prisoners; industrial research, to the problems of managers rather than those of workers; military research, to the problems of generals rather than those of privates. Furthermore, they show how research frequently represents the interests of adults and teachers instead of those of children and students; of men instead of women; of white middle class instead of the lower class, black, and other minorities. This review suggests that sociological research in substantive areas is not free from dominant class and ideological biases. American values of individualism and achievement and the spirit of capitalism have tended to influence the development of academic sociology in the U.S.

The foregoing panoramic view of American sociology makes us realize its increasing diversification in its investigation of numerous and complex social phenomena, and in its multiplicity of methods and theories. This kaleidoscopic nature of American sociology is in major part a reflection of the processes of modernization and rapid technological growth, events, processes - material and ideological, both at home and abroad. American sociology, far from being immune to its nature, seems to have responded to the various critical socio-economic political changes during the past three decades.

VII
Having discussed some of the values, assumptions and controversies related to theories, methods, and substantive areas, let us turn our attention to the nature, content, and role of American sociology in the development of a universal science of sociology. Since its beginnings sociology has been defined as a universal science aimed at developing principles-theories about society, social relations, institutions, groups, processes and problems that transcend spatial and temporal limits. In this sense sociology is to be a universal science like physics, chemistry and biology.

However, American sociology, by and large, has remained ethnocentric, culture bound, and parochial (Hughes, 1961; Marsh, 1967; Webber 1981). As sociology became more empirical, American sociologists tended to study their own society more often than other societies by using methods and theories suitable to American society. Hughes (1961) observes, "We invented ethnocentrism. Now we have fallen in to it." Marsh (1967) points out that many sociological propositions, even though stated as if the generalizations hold true for all societies, have not been rarely tested outside the United States. He emphasizes the need for cross-societal analysis. "Despite the increase in cross-cultural studies," notes Webber, "it remains true that parochialism is the rule in American sociology." Cross-national comparative analysis in doctoral and post- doctoral research in American sociology has been peripheral and insignificant in testing and developing theories.

It seems that sociologists accept the notion of a universal science of sociology but rarely work toward that end. The founding fathers of sociology - Marx, Durkheim, Weber - did undertake cross-cultural comparative analysis of institutions and societies. Contemporary American sociologists, however, have to a great extent failed to comprehend the urgent need for a more substantial cross-societal dimension into sociology. This deficiency in American sociology has serious adverse consequences for the other national sociologies. Later, we will examine the dominant influence of American sociology and its impact on the sociologies of India and Canada.

Meanwhile, it is evident that American sociologists have been culture bound and parochial in their research and theory construction. A large majority of the sociologists of the world are in the U.S. and an overwhelming majority of sociological research and publication activities take place in the U.S. These facts together with very limited cross-national research and predominant influence of American Sociology abroad seem to contradict the aims of a universal science of sociology. The key to altering the present provincial nature of American sociology, it is argued, lies in accepting the centrality of cross-societal comparative analysis, and in bringing about a favourable orientation toward such analysis through changes in emphasis in doctoral training programs and the literature of the field.

The process of globalization of American sociology was accelerated after the end of World War II. The military-industrial complex along with a recognition of America as a major economic political world power led to the American culture and academic imperialism, especially in the non-communist countires.

The dissemination of American sociology abroad was also encouraged by its institutionalization as an academic discipline earlier in the U.S. than anywhere else in the world. According to Shils (1970: 777), American social structure was much more supportive of such a development than those of European countries. The rapid growth of American sociology at home and abroad can be attributed to several factors: the participation of American sociologists in the federal bureaucracy during and after World War II, rapid increase in university enrollment due to post-war baby-boom, and popularity of sociology as a subject, extensive funding by the government and non-government agencies for research and publication, scholarship and training programs for nationals of foreign countries, exchange of scholars, use of American sociological text books (in original or translations) for undergraduate and graduate training abroad, the support of international research by major American foundations such as the Ford, Rockefeller, and Carnegie, or the Fullbright program of the U.S. government, or Unesco sponsored training and research programs. Undoubtedly, the growth of the U.S. as a world power, and the economic, political, and cultural imperialism which accompanied contributed to the dominance of American sociology in several countries of the world.

Gouldner (1970: 22-23) observed, "To much of the world today, sociology is practically synonymous with American sociology." For him American sociology for all practical purposes, is the model of academic sociology throughout the world. In other words, American sociology is being promoted and adopted as if it is a universal science. We have noted earlier, however, that American sociology is culturebound and parochial. Despite important differences in content, approach and practice of sociology in different nations, this predominant influence of American sociology tends to create an American brand of sociology that appears to be considered as a sociology that is universal by some, while others recognize American sociology (in any of its forms) as non- relevant and inimical to the growth of a national sociology, whether it is in India or in Canada. In any event (Birnbaum, 1970), "As the United States became a dominant world power, American sociology's international fortunes rose correspondingly. Where Talcott Parsons and entire generations before, had made scholarly pilgrimages to Europe, did not now younger Europeans (and many older ones, too) take the opposite path?'

A perusal of trend reports on the status of sociology in different countries suggests a differential impact of American sociology on sociologies in, Austrialia and New Zealand[8] (Baldock & Lally, 1976); Britain[9] (Krausz, 1969; Abrams, 1981); Canada (Anderson, 1975; Stolzman & Gamberg, 1975; 1975; Forcese & Richer, 1975; Clark, 1975; Brym, 1986); India (Clinand and Elder, 1965; Chekki, 1978, ICSSR, 1974; Singh, 1979, 1986), Israel[10] (Weller, 1974), Japan[11] (Koyano, 1976), Scandinavia[12] (Kolaja, 1977), and in several other countries (Mohan and Martindale, 1975). Our purpose is to look at the sociologies of India and Canada and the influence of American sociology on these two national sociologies. The reaction of Indian and Canadian sociologies to the academic and professional imperialism of American sociology will also be shown. These two countries - India and Canada - are selected because of their respective geographical distance from and proximity to the U.S., socio-economic and cultural differences, relative newness and antiquity of these societies, similar British and commonwealth ties that have influenced the growth of sociology, and the author's familiarity with India and Canada. Above all, academic sociology in both countries emerged during almost the same period i.e. the second decade of the twentieth century. The next chapter is devoted to a discussion of the process of institutionalization of sociology, impact and relevance of American sociology, critique of national sociology, and a process of indigenization of sociology in India.

Sociology never operates in a social vacuum. It will always absorb and reflect the national culture by which it has been conditioned. In this context, Sociology of India provides a good illustration of a pervasive cultural influence on the nature of sociological work.

CHAPTER 4

BEYOND TRADITIONS & SYNTHESIS AND INDIGENIZATION:

Sociology of India

A common assumption states that sociology has a universally relevant theory, methodology, and an international professional identity. Some sociologists challenge this assumption, and maintain that sociology can only be relevant if its theory and methodology are appropriate to a given socio-cultural milieu of a country. It is in this context that we will examine the nature and consequences of American Sociology - its academic imperialism on sociology in India and in Canada. We are also interested in the issue of relevance of American Sociology as far as sociologies in India and in Canada are concerned and how the latter have reacted to the former. We shall begin, in this chapter, with India and follow it up with Canada in a subsequent chapter.

Since the growth of sociology as a discipline is itself a socio-cultural phenomenon, it would be essential and useful to focus on the socio-cultural factors that have contributed to the development of sociology in India. In our historical and contemporary analysis of the emergence and growth of sociology in India, we shall discuss both the endogenous and exogenous forces that have played a significant role.

Through the centuries, the Indian "Weltanschauung" and ethos, stated in the sacred scriptures, philosophical schools of thought, and religious traditions have been vital elements of the major social institutions, ideals, and values. Indian society has manifested cultural unity amidst diversity, resulting from processes of internal differentiation and importation and adaptation of foreign cultures. Over the ages, continuity of traditions and changes are characteristic of Indian society and culture.

It is demonstrated (Nandy, 1971) that the rise and growth of sociology in India was deeply interwoven with the radical reorientation of the social-intellectual milieu during the Renaissance, the Revolution, and Independence in India. In the early years of the twentieth century, the precursors of sociology such as Arobindo Ghosh, B. K. Sarkar, Tilak, Gokhale, Ranade, Mohandas Gandhi and others tried to link sociology with religion, politics, economics and nationalism. Politivism, values and the non-empirical modes of inquiry with a reformist and at times revolutionary flavor did continue to influence social thought.

In the 1920s with the institutionalization of sociology first at the University of Bombay and later at Lucknow, Calcutta and Mysore universities, Indian sociology adopted theoretical conceptions of society and culture and research methods from the Western sociology and anthropology. Prior to Independence sociology in India was influenced by historical, indological, anthropological, humanistic as well as positivistic approaches.

Saran (1958, 1013-1034) observes that the development of sociological thought in India has been cotemporaneous with her contact with Western culture, resulting in three different responses: (i) a total rejection of the Modern Western civilization and a return to the traditional principles, (ii) attempts at a synthesis of the two cultures, (iii) and a tendency to interpret and justify traditional concepts and institutions in terms of modern rationalistic - positivistic ideas.

The University of Bombay has the unique distinction of pioneering the systematic study of Sociology in India. A separate department to teach and conduct research in sociology was established in 1919, with Professor Patrick Geddes as the first head of the department. G. S. Ghurye[1], who succeeded Geddes in 1924, played a major role in Indian Sociology until his retirement in 1959. His own contributions are primarily in the area of caste, class, tribes, culture and civilization, cities and change. In the sociology graduate program he directed numerous research projects, covering a wide variety of specialties in sociology. K. M. Kapadia devoted his research to the study of marriage, family and kinship, urbanization and change. A. R. Desai's contributions are mainly related to Indian nationalism, rural sociology and problems of development and modernization. Some of the best known sociologists of India such as I. Karve, M. N. Srinivas, I. P. Desai, Y. B. Damle are former students of this school.

The University of Lucknow has been another centre for sociological research and training. R. K. Mukerjee made a sociological study of values and morals and attempted to build a theory of symbolism and a general theory of society. He espoused the ideal of an egalitarian society. In his theory of symbolism he tried to synthesize both Eastern and Western thought. D. P. Mukerji viewed the impact of the West on India as a phase in the process of cultural assimilation and synthesis. He rejected Parson's general theory of action and put forward as the alternative the Hindu theory of man and society free from the Marxian or the Western liberal tradition. D. N. Majumdar, A. K. Saran, S. C. Dube, and T. N. Madan are some of the influential

scholars in Indian sociology and social anthropology associated
with this school.

Men like G. S. Ghurye, R. K. Mukerjee, D. P. Mukerji, to
mention a few, transmitted Western concepts and approaches into
Indian sociology. However, sociology as an academic discipline
and as a research enterprise was confined to a few universities
and as such did not make an impact as a discipline of importance
to be reckoned with.

It was not until 1947, when India attained Independence from
the British rule that sociology, within a changing socio-cultural
milieu, began to experience significant growth. The national
leaders and planners, in their zeal to modernize the country,
perceived the role of sociology, along with the other social
sciences, in the task of national reconstruction and development.
The Universities Grants Commission and the Research Programs
Committee of the Planning Commission gave impetus to sociology.
These federal government agencies provided grants to various
universities and sponsored research on problems of development and
change. This initiative by the government accelerated the pace of
institutionalization and professionalization of sociology in terms
of both teaching and research.

During the post-Independence period (1947-1982) there has
been rapid growth[2] of colleges and universities. An overwhelming
majority of universities - both old and new - have introduced
sociology; and the proportion of students, graduates and
doctorates, and teachers in sociology has increased dramatically.
Moreover, sociology in most universities and colleges in India
today has become independent of other relatively well established
disciplines such as history, economics, political science,
philosophy and psychology. The distinctive sociological approach
and method used by sociologists in the study of social phenomena
and problems is illustrated by the growth of teaching and research
in various branches of sociology. It should be recognized,
however, that in the Indian context it is difficult to distinguish
sociological and social anthropological[3] modes of inquiry and
analysis. Despite the increasing acceptance of the scientific
(positivist) sociological approach, sociology in India has tended
to combine different approaches and perspectives such as the
philosophical, historical-Indological, anthropological and
humanistic.

From the analysis of different aspects of sociology in India
some generalizations can be made about past and recent
developments in Indian sociology. The early development of Indian
sociology during the first half of this century was marked by a
social philosophical approach rather than a strictly sociological
perspective. The social philosophical interpretation of early
Indian sociologists had religious roots in Hinduism. Concepts
from Hinduism gave scholars an encompassing view of society

through which social values could be linked up with ethical and spiritual values (Becker and Barnes, 1961: 1147). The concept of "dharma" for example, is posed as the fundamental law of the cosmos which gives every human being a place in society, where he works out his ultimate destiny with the end purpose of achieving salvation or the realization of the Supreme Being. According to the spiritual ideals of Hinduism, all social life and social organization are directed towards salvation! The social philosophical approach often produced work which was normative and speculative in nature, not based on empirical data. Much of this theoretical writing was devoted to presenting schemes of social evolution (Bottomore, 1962: 98).

This social philosophical trend in Indian sociology has continued into the present. However, a number of new trends have also become evident. Some contemporary Indian sociologists (Saksena, 1962: 95-98) have been calling for a greater emphasis on social philosophies as a reaction to the westernization of Indian sociology, especially in the form of positivism and scientism. These recent social philosophy oriented sociologists seem to have been influenced by the work of D. P. Mukerji and seem to have been concentrated at the University of Lucknow. They are highly critical of western approaches to sociology, and hope to develop sociological theory which is rooted in India's social history and traditional social thought in the form of moral and religious principles which underlie social order.

Indian sociologists have also adopted an Indological approach (Ghurye, Kapadia, Motwani) which seeks to provide an understanding of Indian society through research into ancient Indian texts and scriptures and legal historical documents. The advocates of this historical approach (Clinard and Elder, 1965: 584) emphasize that to understand the present social organization of India, one must be thoroughly familiar with the literature and languages of India's past.

Two noticeable trends in Indian sociology have originated in strong influences from western countries. From the British, Indian sociology developed a trend which is social anthropological. The social anthropological approach stems from the fact that the British, upon whom the Indians were academically dependent before Independence, had made much more progress in social anthropology than they had in sociology (Bottomore, 1962). Social anthropology was given impetus also because of the administrative purposes it could serve for government, such as investigations of tribal peoples, and because of the suitability of anthropological methods for studying many of India's social institutions and problems. This British influence, especially if Indian scholars have been trained in Britain, has led to an emphasis on rural studies while many urban social phenomena remain inadequately researched, although this rural emphasis may be justifiable considering that a large majority of India's population lives in villages.

Since Independence, American influences have been more instrumental in charting the course of Indian sociology. American influences are felt more in the areas of methodology and technique (Bottomore, 1965). Following the stress on empiricism found in American sociology, some Indian scholars have begun to use the idea of testing hypotheses, and have adopted statistical tools. Along with American empiricism has come the notion that sociological investigations should be objective. The acceptance or rejection of objectivity as a desirable goal for research has generated much debate. A number of prominent Indian sociologists, especially those with the philosophical tendencies, are of the opinion that because "man's behaviour and experience cut across many dimensions and metaphysics provides the law of his living, it's metaphysical speculations as regards man and society... that furnishes the ultimate postulates of all social sciences and social action" (Mukerjee, 1958). R. N. Saksena (1961) believed that the philosophical elements of Indian sociology are necessary in that they provide a continuum between the past and present.

During (1947-1972) the first twenty-five years after Independence, sociology in India has expanded quite dramatically. The number of universities teaching sociology have increased greatly as well as the number of students enrolled (see, Appendix) in sociology courses, the number of colleges and universities teaching sociology programes, and the number of M.A. and Ph.D. degrees awarded has increased. The publication of sociological researches has also greatly increased in conjunction with the increases in the number of Indian sociologists. It appears that despite influences of American empiricism there has been little use of computers and quantitative or statistical methods. Little theoretical development or methodological innovation has taken place, although a few ideas more recently are being developed which are uniquely suited to the Indian context. Possibly because of the vastness of India, and probably because of lack of initiative and funding for macro level research projects, most studies have taken a microscopic, rather than a macroscopic view, while most of the work which has been done at the micro level has not been organized or synthesized to yield generalizations for all of India. Thus, comparative studies have hardly been conducted either between India and other countries or among regions in India (Chekki, 1978).

The development of Indian sociology was classified (Mukherjee 1977, 1979: 319-332) under a time-sequence of 1920-40, and the 1950s, 1960s, and 1970s with the 'pioneers', 'modernizers', 'insiders', and 'pace-makers' versus 'nonconformists' playing distinctive roles in the respective periods. It is stated that the pioneers' approach was synoptic and their theoretical formulations, though not precise enough, had a good deal of inductive power to generalize from a multi-dimensional comprehension of social reality in the historical, contemporary and futuristic perspectives.

For the modernizers social change was an ideology, not only a matter for theoretical comprehension. The research orientation of the modernizers was essentially pragmatic and explained social change in modern India in terms of the complementary processes of 'Sanskritization' and 'westernization'.

The modernizers could not produce better, or even significant sociological theory on the basis of a comprehensive appraisal of social reality in India. Moreover, Mukherjee notes that the deductive and simplistic methodology of the dominant section of the modernizers produced a fragmentary or distorted appraisal of social reality. The methodology of the other section of the modernizers which followed the theory and practice dominating American rural sociology in the 1950s, was sophisticated, but not necessarily efficient in the Indian context because of its uncritical acceptance. In any event, the modernizers, though they helped to considerably broaden the data base of Indian sociology, did not succeed in producing a better understanding of social reality.

During this period sociologists exhibited various value preferences and research orientations. The structural-functional approach has been a dominant mode of analysis. A few sociologists such as Mukherjee, R., Desai, A.R., Saran, A.K., have followed a Marxist[1] approach for sociological analysis.

In the 1960s, influenced by the outlook of the behavioural science as then prevalent in the U.S.A., sociologists adopted a holistic approach and participated in interdisciplinary research with other social scientists. The 1960s appeared in a large measure to be a continuation of the 1950s in the mode and manner of social research, but with more specialization of the discipline, diversification of its thematic content in the Indian context, and the adoption of appropriate methodology for micro-sociology.

Despite changes in the 1960s, the optimism of the 1950s regarding the ushering in of change in India through rapid economic growth was found to be an illusion. There was also a growing realization among some sociologists that the kind of sociology advocated and accepted since the 1950s was not adequate to understand the dynamics of Indian society. In place of an imitative development of Indian sociology, the indigenization of Indian sociology was demanded not merely in form but also in content. The Marxist approach has not been well received by the policy makers and by a majority of social scientists. However, a group of young sociologists aims toward making Indian sociology effective in changing reality.

In the 1960s and 1970s sociologists in India seem to have been influenced by both capitalist and socialist ideologies. During these two decades increasing numbers of sociological researches were sponsored and supported by the Planning Commission and the Universities Grants Commission to propose and/or evaluate various government[5] initiated programs of development and change. Indian sociologists tended to follow either a value neutral, scientific objectivity stance or a value committed action orientation. A few sociologists, however, tried to combine both these approaches.

In the late 1970s, it appears that there has been a better coordination of theory and research than ever attained before. This is exemplified by (a) more critical concept formation, (b) search for new avenues to appraise social reality, and (c) reconsideration of the modes of studying the society which were advocated by the pioneers.

III
As a result of the unprecedented growth of sociology as an academic discipline in the post-Independence era, a number of problems arose. Universities and colleges experienced the need for qualified teachers, with a shortage of funds for hiring sociologists, and the need for indigenous course materials in Indian languages, and had to contend with the problems of medium of instruction.

In evaluating the present status of teaching sociology in India it is observed (Rao, M.S.A. et. al. 1978) that there are bright as well as dark spots. While some post-graduate university departments have been the centres of innovation in teaching sociology many others remain below standard and the organization of teaching at different levels needs more careful planning.

Sociology courses at the undergraduate level are reported to be too wide and descriptive, with substantive courses not adequately related to sociological concepts. Research methodology courses both at the undergraduate and graduate levels are heavily biased toward survey and quantitative techniques. A need is felt to strike a balance between the quantitative, non-quantitative and the logical aspects. It is suggested that the courses offered at the M.A. level should be more systematically interlinked and the teaching of courses should be related to the conditions and problems of Indian society and culture.

Regarding the modernization of syllabi in sociology, Indian sociologists have arrived at a consensus that the cognitive contents of the courses must primarily be grounded in the Indian concrete reality and its history. Another area of consensus is that at higher levels the courses should be more diversified with greater theoretical and substantive contents emphasizing regional, national and international comparative approaches. Indian sociologists have also recognized the undesirability of a completely standardized uniform structure of syllabi for all regions of the country, although a basic minimum is considered to be necessary.

With increased introduction of sociology at several universities and colleges and with rapid increases in the enrollment of students for sociology courses, the problems of teaching sociology have surfaced in the profession, especially in the 1970s. Teaching is recognized as a crucial instrument in the transmission of sociological knowledge and skills. Sponsored by the Universities Grants Commission, rather than by the Indian Sociological Society, several committees comprising sociologists have looked at the problems of teaching sociology and have noted that the content and quality of teaching is dependent upon the kind of courses taught, capabilities of teachers, availability of teaching materials, the medium of instruction, the examination and evaluation system, student motivations, and the job market.
Thus it is obvious that sociology in India has reached a stage where sociologists manifest professional concerns by taking active part in the formulation of policies regarding course content and format, standards for hiring sociologists, and admission of students. A need for teaching materials that are relevant to the Indian social milieu and/or derived from social researches in India, is being felt. This need is more pronounced where teaching materials in Indian languages are concerned. Likewise, Indian sociologists have tried to re-examine teaching methods and have been experimenting with a medium of regional language instruction in different parts of the country. The U.G.C. Committees have recommended seminars, workshops and exchange programs for faculty, production of teaching materials in regional languages and the restructuring of the examination and evaluation system for significant improvements in teaching-learning sociology in India.

IV
The trends and problems in sociological research and publication are not underestimated. Though there are research facilities at the university level, they can hardly be compared with those that exist in American universities. At the college level, research facilities, for all practical purposes, can rarely be identified. This situation is further worsened by heavy teaching loads. Even at the university level, however, there is no system of sabbatical leave for research. The available research grants and fellowships are considered to be inadequate to meet the needs of researchers in their research and publication activities. Though the profession of sociology has its own

national association - the Indian Sociological Society - having its official publication: **Sociological Bulletin,** the publication outlets, especially in terms of journals, are rather limited in the context of a tremendous increase, despite the porblems listed above, in the number of sociologists and their research output.

Characteristics of a society's culture can affect the perspectives and methods employed and selection of substantive areas for research. Some topics may be more or even uniquely stressed because social reality (Lazarsfeld, 1973) brings them to the attention of sociologists. The selection of topics and emphasis on specific areas for research varies from country to country because of differences in cultural traditions. Sometimes a subject matter finds preferential treatment because the personal interest of a prominent scholar, or because an institution happens to exist which facilitates the flow of work in a specific direction.

The nature, content, and direction of sociology in India has been influenced by its cultural diversity, traditions, institutional establishments, and prominent scholars' personal interests. Not only theoretical perspectives and substantive areas but also the research methods selected by sociologists have the imprint of their culture. For instance, Indian sociologists have long stressed the use of participant observation methods, despite the influence of American survey research methods, because the distinction between sociology and social anthropology is blurred by virture of the nature of the society in India and British influence.

During the first twenty-five years following Independence, in Indian Sociology the most highly researched areas have been culture and social structure, rural sociology, social differentiation and stratification, family-kinship and socialization, social change and economic development (Chekki, 1978). A large number of village community studies were undertaken by both American and Indian scholars during the 1950s and 1960s. These village studies are primarily descriptive ethnographic accounts of caste, family, and the impact of change. The method of research has been mostly participant observation, interview; also questionnaires to a limited extent. No significant effort seems to have been made to codify these micro studies or focus on problems of rural development at the macro level.

Nationwide team research, using national samples, on problems of national importance are very few, if any. Despite priority research areas established by the Indian Council of Social Science Research, much remains to be researched in areas such as inequality, poverty, population and family planning, caste and communal tensions, education, political processes, welfare planning and administration, and the impact of development programs. Furthermore, so far the nature of the sociological research in India appears to be primarily empirical without adequate theoretical development. The publicly funded social science research organizations like the ICSSR, according to Varma (1979), "have failed to give the declared bold new direction to our highly Americanized social science research in terms of problem selection, analytic frame and social purpose." Research projects on trivial and irrelevant topics are thought to be a waste of public money serving the interests of the ruling class and encouraging careerism among bourgeois academics.

Although there has been considerable effort in training young Indian sociologists in the use of statistical-quantitative methods in sociological research, there is not enough evidence of its use in sociological analysis. Books, journal articles or research reports by sociologists have hardly made extensive use of quantitative research methods. It is evident that Indian sociology has not yet achieved a balance between quantitative and qualitative research.

Indian sociologists engaged in research have to face several problems. The appalling poverty of funds for research, at least until the beginning of the 1970s, explains in major part the reason for limited sociological research activity.[6] This situation has considerably changed with the establishment (in 1969) of the Indian Social Science Research Council as a major agency for funding social science research. There are, however, no big trusts or foundations established by philanthropic businesses or industrial families. With funding opportunities being limited, sociologists have to limit applications for research grants to federal government supported funding agencies such as the I.C.S.S.R. and the U.G.C.

The heavy teaching load, absence of sabbaticals, lack of funds, complex bureaucratic procedural delays, lack of sufficient recognition for research and publications by university administration, and lack of adequate library and secretarial facilities still act as hurdles in the research process. The idea that the production of knowledge is an important role of universities is not yet well established. Moreover, the bureaucratic rigidity of universities seems to discourage many younger sociologists from engaging in research.

If one succeeds in overcoming these obstacles and embarks upon a research project, the sponsoring agency, the department head, and sometimes politicians exert direct or indirect pressure with regard to the scope and the method of inquiry, the place of inquiry, and the publication of the results of research. In some research issues or areas of strategic importance it is reported (Madan, 1967) that the government of India is concerned about national security, political or religious tensions. Since the granting agencies tend to support research dealing with problems of development and change it seems that most researchers submit proposals focusing on socio-economic problems and change rather than on theoretical issues or fundamental research of substantive areas that are not directly linked to development problems.

The elite sociologists who hold positions of power in the academic community exert influence in reviewing research proposals, and articles and manuscripts submitted for publication, in hiring sociologists for faculty positions, etc. They act as gatekeepers in deciding what kind of research to be published and what should be withheld from publication. Obviously intellectual and personal biases of a few influential sociologists will shape the course of published sociology. Sociological journals in India are very few and they are also controlled and edited by a few. Usually the editor has discretion to accept or reject an article. By and large, with a few exceptions, there is no system of anonymous evaluation of papers by referees. The authors are not informed of the basis for rejection and do not receive comments for revision.

During the past two decades (1960-1980) there has been considerable doctoral research in sociology. In selection of topics/problems for research, and in theoretical approach, research methods and analysis of data there seems to be a tendency on the part of department heads or research supervisors to impose on doctoral candidates their own research interests and value commitments.

Ethical constraints and dilemmas are experienced by researchers when their own caste or religious values conflict with that of certain groups and communities that a sociologist is investigating. Madan (1967) reports several such instances. Another ethical problem faced by researchers concerns acknowledgement and coauthorship of journal articles and books, especially when students and research assistants or colleagues have a major input in to research.

Despite these political pressures and ethical constraints, Indian sociologists have enjoyed considerable freedom to undertake research. Furthermore, sociologists have sometimes criticised government policies and programs even when research projects were financed by government agencies.

V

The rapid increase in teaching and research activities has contributed to the professionalization of the discipline. The Indian Sociological Society came into existence in 1951 through the initiative of G.S. Ghurye of the University of Bombay. In 1955 the Indian Sociological Association was formed. In 1967 this

Association was merged with the Indian Sociological Society. The **Sociological Bulletin** is the official journal of the Indian Sociological Society, which had a membership of 500 in 1971. The Journal's total circulation was over 1,000 copies in 1971. The I.S.S. has been holding annual conferences though in recent years it has been meeting less frequently.

Besides universities and colleges, there are several research centres and institutes where sociological research funded by government, industry, and the I.S.C.C.R has been in progress. The publication of sociological journals and books has also increased, but this is not in proportion to the increase in the number of sociologists and research projects. For instance, **Sociological Bulletin**, after three decades of its existence, publishes only two issues per year, lags behind in its schedule of publication, and has neither substantially increased the number of its printed pages nor its frequency. Less than 1/4th of the published books in sociology are reviewed in this journal. The number of articles, academic debates and discussions, and professional commentaries are extremely limited. There seems to be a great need to turn this journal into a quarterly publication, thereby providing more space for publication of research papers of both a substantive and theoretical nature, as well as for adequate coverage of a larger number of book reviews and commentaries.

The profession of sociology in India has been facing a number of problems: (i) credibility crisis, (ii) crises of knowledge dissemination. Atal (1976: 130) has noted that because of heavy reliance on textbooks published in the U.S.A., sociology in India is treated as the "ideology of capitalism", and "supporter of the status quo." He further states that critics of the discipline - both insiders and outsiders - single out the structural-functional approach as the key culprit. In its place, two different brands of historical approach are recommended: Indological and Marxian. A committed sociology has also been advocated. Empiricism and survey research are under attack as well.

In terms of knowledge generation, the sociological research enterprise in India is rather limited in quantity compared to large scale research projects in the U.S. with millions of dollars devoted for them. Many sociologists in India seem to lack motivation for research because of a university climate that is not generally conducive to knowledge creation. During the 1970s this situation has somewhat improved because of the policies and programs implemented by the I.C.S.S.R. However, the fact remains that the production of sociological knowledge in India has not yet attained the same stage as it has in the United States.

Despite a growing interest in Sociology, the problem of dissemination of sociological knowledge to the public at large and to government planners-administrators, the experts in the field of health, agriculture, engineering, justice and law enforcement, religious and social welfare organizations, and funding agencies in particular remains to be accomplished. The Indian Sociological Society, unlike the American Sociological Association, has not been a strong lobbying group.

Many Indian sociologists seem to be content in their role primarily as teachers and secondarily as researchers and have hardly made efforts to communicate to the public through the press, radio and television. This is in sharp contrast to their American colleagues. In fact, several well known American sociologists have contributed their skills, services and time to 'sell' sociology to the American public. Sociologists' participation in the **Voice of America** lecture series, writings in the **New York Times** and other newspapers and magazines, television interviews, and reporting of sociological survey research results in popular magazines have made sociology almost a household word. In India very limited effort, if any, is being made in this direction. This is probably because of a lack of consensus on the professional role of sociologists in India.

The process of socialization of a new generation of sociologists in India is also beset with problems. As noted earlier, the paucity of research and consequent lack of instructional material based on empirical research in India has necessitated a heavy reliance on American textbooks in colleges and universities.

A dramatic increase in the enrollment of students for sociology, their varied background, the lack of qualified and competent teachers, fossilized syllabi, lack of indigenous instructional materials, the problems of communicating sociology through regional language, and emphasis on coursework and examination at post-graduate levels have all contributed to a state of affairs where "they have many M.A.'s in Sociology but very few sociologists" (Atal, 1976). Obviously, this situation calls for significant changes in the system of recruitment and training of sociologists.

A committee of sociologists, sponsored by the Universities Grants Commission (Rao et al, 1978), examined the status of teaching of sociology and made a number of recommendations: involvement of concerned teachers and students in the formulation of courses, faculty improvement programs, innovations in teaching methods, production of teaching materials in regional languages, restructuring of examination and evaluation system, raising the minimum eligibility conditions for students to enter sociology, and making courses more relevant by incorporating applied research in the Indian context. It is yet to be seen to what extent these recommendations will be implemented to bring about major changes

in the existing system of socialization of a new breed of
sociologists.

During the 1947-1985 period, sociology in India has tended to
achieve greater academic status, in that not only have many more
universities and colleges introduced sociology, but also sociology
appears to have established its disciplinary identity by
increasingly dissociating itself from other social sciences.
Moreover, sociological research on the problems of development in
independent India has made the federal government aware of the
role of sociology in planning and change. Indian sociologists
have been engaged in research on the problems of urbanization,
industrialization, population, tribal and rural development,
inequality, and various other changing aspects of Indian society.

As far as external intellectual influences are concerned,
there has been a major shift from the British to the American
sociological traditions.   In addition, the French, German and
Marxian intellectual traditions have had some influence on Indian
sociology. However, let us now turn our attention to the dominant
influence of American sociology on sociology in post-Independent
India.

VI
The impact of American sociology on Indian sociology during
the past three decades (1950-1980) has been quite significant.
Since the mid 1950s increasing exchange of scholars between the
U.S. and India, increased use of American sociology textbooks,
together with aid for research from Ford, Rockefeller and other
American foundations have had their influence on the growth of
sociology in India.

Several Indian scholars, either trained in the U.S. or
exposed to American sociology, have been responsible for the
diffusion of American sociology in India.   The dominant
theoretical framework, i.e., structural-functionalism that was
prevalent in the U.S. during the 1950s and early 1960s was
readily accepted by many sociologists in India. Likewise, the
characteristic features of American sociology such as a heavy
emphasis on empirical research and quantitative research methods
were emulated by Indian sociologists. This apparent dependence of
Indian sociology on American sociology makes Uberoi (1968:   122)
wonder why the colonial relations, broken in politics, persist in
science. I. P. Desai (1981) points outs that during the 1950s
and early 1960s, for an academic position, a foreign degree, or
even a stay abroad without any degree was considered more
acceptable by the universities.   Such people filled up many
positions in the university departments.   He called these
foreign-returned sociologists a 'priestly' category, not in a
derogatory but in a functional sense.

Namboodiri (1980: 285-288) also observes that in the post 1950 period, Indian sociology became increasingly 'Westernized' by accepting structual-functionalism as the best guide for analysis of data and with the proliferation of American collaboration in empirical research. Several Indian sociologists, however, have been quite critical of such wholesale acceptance of American sociological theories[7] and research methods without considering their relevance to Indian social and cultural milieu.

From 1960 onwards, Indian sociologists (Singh, 1978: 115-118) turned their attention away from the micro-sociological model to comparative and macro-sociological models, in order to free themselves from external influences and develop their own model of thinking about reality. Marxist and Neo-Marxian theoretical orientations began to influence Indian sociological thought.

During the 1970s American sociology continued to influence Indian sociology, but in a more selective way than it did initially. This selective reception of sociological knowledge from the U.S. and other external sources is in accordance with India's tradition of adoption and modification of foreign cultural elements without losing its own identity. As such, Indian sociology, despite the American influence since Independence, has retained its unique character.

Indian sociology, for the past thirty-five years (1947-1982), has been growing as a mixture of various endogenous and exogenous intellectual traditions. The substantive content of sociology has ranged from tribal, peasant to urban-industrial communities reflecting diverse social realities in India. It is evident that the multi-dimensional nature of Indian sociology is characteristic of its multi-faceted socio-cultural environment.

While American sociology in the 1970s experienced considerable competition, controversy, debate and confrontation among different theoretical schools and research methodologies, Indian sociology has with a few exceptions, remained less conflict-ridden than American sociology. Instead of ideological-theoretical-methodological controversies and battles, what we find in contemporary Indian sociology is a tolerance for different perspectives and a trend toward synthesis of various kinds of sociologies prevalent in India and abroad. Obviously, this process has not contributed to a sociology of India that can be recognized as a photocopy of American sociology.

Indeed, some Indian sociologists have advocated a distinct sociology for India with its own concepts, theories, and methods of inquiry. Others have maintained that Indian sociology is distinct only in terms of its focus, and research emphasis. It is believed (Nandy, 1971: 145) that with the development of a universalistic and synthetic sociology, with a place in it for diverse patterns of sociology, Indian sociology can unfold its creative best, and also contribute its share to the development of a world sociology.

The trends of the 1970s do indicate that Indian sociology has been developing theoretical concerns (Singh, 1979: 116-118) and comparative perspectives by using native categories and testing several hypotheses derived from Weberian, Marxist and other theoretical paradigms. These theoretical orientations are being applied to the Indian social reality rather innovatively and in this process Indian sociologists are generating new theoretical insights by challenging classical sociological theories.

Furthermore, Singh (1986), while providing an overview of the developments in Indian sociology during the period 1970-1985, noted the extent to which theoretical and cognitive systems of sociology are socially conditioned. This study shows the social conditioning of the discipline as reflected in the choice of paradigms, substantive areas of research, definitions of the context of relevance and the acute sensitivity to using the framework of history and tradition in the interpretation and construction of social reality.

Another notable trend during the seventies has involved a series of studies on the problems of the disadvantaged groups such as tribes and lower castes (eg: ex-untouchables) and their education, unemployment and poverty, women's studies, studies of inequality, etc., sponsored by the I.C.S.S.R. These studies have provided useful data for planning. In theoretical terms there has been considerable attention focused on alternate models of development in the Indian context. The I.C.S.S.R. has also sponsored a series of training courses in research methodology and has provided fellowships, research and publication grants to scholars.

During the 1970s the number of American scholars engaged in research in India has declined. The government of India discovered that the CIA and other agencies of the U.S. government had not only been supporting research but also using research data for political and military purposes. Consequently, the government of India imposed restrictions on American sponsored research and researchers.

VII

Despite the influence of American sociology, Indian sociology manifests certain distinct patterns of growth. The following comparative analysis aims at providing a brief review of trends in the growth of sociology in the U.S. and in India. This review highlights some of the similarities and differences that prevail in the content and direction of the growth of Indian sociology and American sociology.

Both Indian and American national schools of sociology were quite theoretically oriented in their earliest stages of development. These theoretical orientations were characterized by a deductive approach or one where generalizations were not formulated on the basis of sets of empirical data. In both countries the theories were social- philosophical in nature, and were concerned with social change or social evolution.

While sociology in America and in India were influenced by particular socio-religious milieus, those spiritual influences had different effects on the discipline's development in each country. In America, Protestant evangelism tended to produce a brand of sociology which was oriented towards social problems, social reforms, and social work. Hinduism, in contrast, tended to make Indian sociology more philosophical and rooted in religious values and spiritualism. It is this orientation in Indian sociology which perhaps had made it somewhat unconcerned with certain social problems in earlier years. For example, criminology did not receive much attention (Becker and Barnes, 1961) partly because of the unique attitude towards criminals, who are members of castes or tribes among whom crime is a hereditary calling, just as other forms of employment such as carpentry or farming.

The religious influences in both countries however, were expressed through a belief among sociologists that they had some right, if not a duty, to insist on social reforms (Faris, 1945: 544). In American sociology this orientation, which was inherent within it a number of value judgements, was later met with the advent of neo-positivistic empiricism. American empiricism aspired for objectivity, and to that end saw sociology only as indicating the consequences of alternate social policies, not specifying which of the consequences were more desirable (Valien and Valien, 1957: 86). In contrast, while some Indian sociologists have followed these American tendencies, another group has continued to stress that Indian sociology should not and cannot be value neutral, because it is believed that social institutions cannot be understood unless they are related to Hinduism and its ideas of life's mission. The truth of the evolutionary and spiritual outlook on life must be accepted before attempts are made to interpret and analyse Indian society. Once sociologists have accepted these truths then they have, in some case, become social commentators. For example, it is stated (Suda, 1967: 27) that: "Today the world is too much with us, we remain immersed in competitive economic activities till death claims us, and thereby fail to render unto God things that belong to Him. The practical disappearance of the last two stages of life has been mainly responsible for our rational decay." Such statements are based on a belief in Hinduism and are value-loaded.

Both Indian and American sociologists have tended to conduct studies at the microscopic level. This may be the case simply because of the vastness of their respective countries and the limitations imposed by sociology's methods of data collection such as interviews and questionnaires administered to representative sample members. The empiricism of both national schools of sociology and the microscopic perspectives have tended to make recent developments in sociology quite weak in theory. However, in both countries, this theoretical weakness has been recognized, and attempts are being made to improve the situation. Indian sociologists are especially at a disadvantage in theory building because in the past, much has been borrowed from the West and applied to Indian society. Such procedures have been questioned because the assumptions which underlie western philosophies do not coincide with Indian assumptions (Clinard and Elder, 1965: 583). Indian sociologists are therefore now faced with the challenge of developing theories which are applicable to Indian society instead of relying on western theories. Indian sociologists may find some insights in this area from the historical sociological works which can provide the time perspective or continuity which is needed for theories of social change.

Although Indian sociology has maintained its earlier philosophical leanings, empiricism has remained another dominant trend. Indian empiricism, however, is different from the American approach. American empiricism has been characterized by an emphasis on quantification and objectivity, while Indian empiricism has remained quite non- quantitative. Sociological empiricism in India has been heavily influenced by social anthropology. Thus, many studies collect primary data through field surveys, not necessarily using interviews or questionnaires, and do not analyse the data quantitatively because field survey data is not as readily quantified as the data by an interview or questionnaire. The non- quantitative aspect of Indian sociology has been accompanied by a lack of computer facilities, in contrast to the American use of computers and "sophisticated" mathematical techniques. The lack of computer facilities in India is related to the general lack of funds within universities. More recently, however, most universities are being equipped with computers. Other factors such as heavy teaching duties and limited resources for research have also contributed to meagre research activity. This has meant that Indian sociology has not been able to increase in research productivity as rapidly as the Americans, even though much progress has been made in India during the 1970-1980 period.

In both countries, closed alliances have developed between sociolgy and other social sciences, in India, with social anthropology, and in America, with social psychology. These interdisciplinary ties have not entirely paralleled one another in both countries. American sociologists have their differences with psychologists over the scope of social psychology, while Indian sociologists and social anthropologists appear to be more united in scope and method. This situation could prevail in India because many aspects of Indian society, such as rural and tribal institutions, provide a common meeting ground for sociologists and anthropologists.

Currently, Indian sociology stands apart from American sociology. Conscious efforts are being made to identify non-Indian influences and evaluate their worth for the study of Indian society, with the view in mind that Indian sociologists must develop some individuality. The general assumption now seems to be that borrowing from the West can be more detrimental than beneficial. On the other hand, American sociology appears to have acquired, quite understandably, greater maturity and definition, so that the discipline is much more secure or on a surer footing both in academic and non-academic settings.

VIII
Sociologists from India and abroad have advocated different kinds of sociologies, or at least seem to have different conceptions of what Indian sociology is or ought to be.

Under the title 'For a Sociology of India', Dumont and Pocock (1957: 7-22) initiated a discussion presenting a distinct view of sociology of India in the hope of eliciting comments from colleagues. In their opinion, the first condition for a sound development of a sociology of India is found in the establishment of the proper relation between it and classical Indology. While claiming, in principle, that a sociology of India lies at the point of confluence of Sociology and Indology, they referred to a small band of scholars who have combined both effectively. Dumont and Pocock postulate that India is one and it can best be understood as a single system of ideas or values through an analsysis of the values of Hinduism.

Bailey (1959: 88-101) disagrees with Dumont and Pocock on their conception of Indian sociology, as a form of culturology that is too narrow a perspective. Bailey is interested in the study of Indian social phenomena from the comparative point of view. The debate for a sociology of India revolves around several theoretical, methodological, and substantive issues. For instance, Damle (1964) makes a plea for the use of the Parsonian frame of reference. Madan (1966: 9-16) raises the question: Why is it that Indian sociologists have not been interested in examining the theoretic assumptions underlying their studies? He thinks that the Indian sociologist has been a victim of history (the colonial situation) and of positivist orientation of Western sociology leading to his peculiar intellectual sloth. For him (1967) there cannot be many sociologies, but sociological understanding must take account of social specificity. Moreover, it is recognized that the Indian sociologist has not made a significant contribution to the development and refinement of sociological concepts.

This deficiency makes Uberoi (1968: 122-123) wonder why the "colonial relation", broken in politics, persists in science. He asserts: "Until we can concentrate on decolonization, learn to nationalize our problems and take our poverty seriously, we shall continue to be both colonial and unoriginal. A national school, avowed and conscious, can perhaps add relevance, meaning and potency to our science; continued assent to the international system cannot."

A common thread that binds a group of sociologists in this debate is a belief that the patterns of Indian social structure are so unique that they require a special sociology of India, asking different questions but using similar Western methods to answer them (Unnithan et al (eds.), 1967). Kantowsky (1969: 128-131) while expressing critical comments with reference to Indian sociology notes that the fact that "Indian sociologists quote Talcott Parsons does not prove that the structural-functional analysis has stood the test within the Indian milieu. Rather, it indicates an adaptive process by many Indian social scientists to the rules of the dominant caste within the Euro-American social science game. He asserts that studies in developing countries should try to make their relevance clear, not only in regard to practical questions but also to the theoretical problems of the social sciences in general. For Kantowsky it is impossible to make any general social scientific statement without proper reference to intercultural data. Therefore, there is no need to distinguish the "sociology of developing countries" from the "sociology of industrial countries". In the same vien it is maintained (Atal, 1976: 132) that Indian sociology is distinctive only in terms of its focus and research emphasis. The strategy of parochialization is not a proper response to the parochial sociology of the West.

While recognizing the existential roots of scientific propositions and paradigms intuitively formulated by scientists, Singh (1970: 140-144) thinks of the possibility of an Indian sociology based on concepts and propositions derived from the study of Indian society. However, "the sociological propositions which would form the basis of Indian or any other national sociology would of course have less theoretic power than those of general sociology".

Narain (1971: 131-135) observes that in having a history of its own, surely Indian society is not unique, and he seems to imply that there is no need for a sociology of India with its own concepts, theories, and methods. He agrees with Bailey (1959) that Indian society, granting all its uniqueness, must still be seen in the context of the general principles of sociology. Because of the inadequacy of the methods of natural science in dealing with meanings, values, and behavior of humans, he hopes to bring about a fruitful marriage between the scientific and humanistic approaches in sociology.

Ahmed (1972: 172-178) demonstrates the pronounced tendency among sociologists to equate Hindu society with India and neglect of other religious groups and sects. He argues that greater attention must be paid to non-Hindu societies if the aim is to build a comprehensive sociology of India. "Until then", he notes, "we may have Hindu, Muslim, or Christian sociologies, but hardly a sociology of India."

In the mid 1960's, the seminar on 'Sociology for India' raised the question: should sociology for India be an altogether independent discipline both in theory and method and apply itself to the analysis of the typical social phenomena of the Indian society, or should it be a general body of concepts and theory with the help of which the general as well as specific problems of any social phenomena, Indian or non-Indian, could be analyzed and interpreted? The papers presented and the discussion that followed challenged and rejected the possibility of a typical or particularistic Indian sociology.

However, Saksena (1962) maintains that Indian sociology cannot be divorced from metaphysical thinking and it cannot be entirely objective in its content. It is also suggested (Srivastava, 1966) that Indian sociology should focus its attention on problems of basic conceptualization within the frame of Indian social data. The dearth of concepts applicable to Indian social phenomena is noted (Mohan, 1975) and 'middle range' studies instead of 'grand generalizations' are considered to be more adequate to the empirical reality of Indian social phenomena.

The cultural diversity of India is reflected in Indian sociology. There is a lack of consensus among Indian sociologists as to whether sociology in India should be historical-indological, empirical, functional, dialectic, micro- or macroscopic, and so on. The advocates of sociological particularism aim at developing concepts, theories, and methods arising out of and relevant to social reality in India. The advocates of sociological universalism tend to accept theories and methods from the Western countries.

Borrowing from the West - primarily the U.S. - it is believed, (Rao and Rao, 1977: 259-63) fosters intellectual dependency and 'Indian sociology degenerates into replicative, deductive, intellectual enterprise; an exercise merely of testing the cross-cultural validity of the Western models and formulations rather than inductive initiatives leading to independent conceptual formulations springing from close observations of indigenous phenomena'. Furthermore, it is argued that this task of merely testing the cross-cultural validity of the Western models reduces the Indian sociological community to the position of a mass consumer of Western sociology, by providing a market for its output.

Indian sociology, Unnithan argues, must follow an integrative 'middle path' between 'sociological universalism' and 'sociological regionalism', adopting sociological concepts to the peculiarities of Indian social phenomena. Namboodiri (1980: 285-288) recognizes some of the unique characteristics of Indian society such as the heavy concentration of population in villages, with a caste structure and a joint family system and spiritual and moral ideas like Dharma, Karma, Moksha, etc. which should be taken into account when studying social processes in India. But for him it does not follow that in order for sociology to be concerned with history and cultural contexts, sociological methods and models have to be society-specific.

This debate and controversy surrounding the nature of Indian sociology tends to form three different camps of sociologists: (a) those who advocate distinct concepts, theories, and methods appropriate for the study of Indian society, (b) those who wish to consider sociology as a universal science with common concepts, theories and methods that can be used to study any society including Indian, (c) those who favour integration and adaptation of sociological concepts, theories and methods to the peculiarities of Indian phenomena.

As a reaction to a Western, especially American, sociological view of social phenomena that has prevailed in India, a movement of indigenization has been set in motion, aimed at the interpretation and understanding of social reality with due regard for the historical and cultural specificities. For Madan (1979: 3) "indigenization stands for the effort to cultivate self awareness, to see ourselves not as others would see us, or not only as others would see us, but as we may also see ourselves." Here the outsider's view of reality alone is considered inadequate, and at times distorted, because the problem lies in the Western view of scientific or objective knowledge of human behavior at the cost of its meaning and significance for the actors themselves.

The issue is not merely one of a dichtomy between 'outsider's vs. insiders's view of reality posed by Merton (1972). "The outsider's view," in the case of India as reported by Madan, "was enthroned as the exclusively valid vision. It became the truth."

A relationship of dependency extended from the political areas to the intellectual circles.

In this context, indigenization is neither meant to be parochialization nor a means to an end. Its goal is the self conscious definition of research-worthy questions and the enrichment of the social sciences as instruments of general understanding and of practical action in historically specific situations: theoretical universals must illumine concrete problems. This indigenization movement seems to incorporate a new vision of mankind - a non exploitative relationship among humans and a harmonious relationship between humans and the biosphere.

American sociology is considered (Varma, 1979) to be largely regressive in imparting a conservative and superficially empiricist influence on social research in India. Therefore, social scientists in India are asked to take a clearly anti-imperialistic stance and devote their energies to the emancipation of the masses from the shackles of colonialism and neo-colonialism. Furthermore, it is argued that social inquiry should be relevant to problems of the masses and to the enrichment of life in India. These critical reflections and new directions seem to be the basis for Dube (1977) to comment that "there has been a visible unease within Indian sociology about its direction and purpose."

The foregoing analysis of the process of institutionalization of sociology in India suggests that the discipline has developed beyond its traditional moorings. While exposed to internal socio-cultural processes as well as external forces, especially to the hegemonic influence of American sociology, sociology in India has tried to retain its unique sociological tradition of a synthetic approach in theory, method, and substantive research. More importantly, sociology in India has reacted to external intellectual domination through an indigenization movement. Canadian sociology, to be discussed in the next chapter, provides another example of a different kind manifesting varied responses to its socio cultural milieu both within and outside.

CHAPTER 5

THE QUEST
FOR RELEVANCE AND NATIONALITY:
Canadian Sociology

I

Canada and the United States, in sharp contrast to India, share a common continent. "Superficially", as Porter observes, "Canada seems much like the United States. Canadians use the same products, appear to go to the same kind of schools, read largely the same periodicals, and watch the same television programs." In this context, the strong cultural similarity between English-speaking Canada and the United States cannot be ignored.

Despite socio-economic and cultural differences between India and Canada, there are some common historical and political influences that both countries share. The impact of British culture and consequent emergence of similar educational, and political institutions, and administrative system along with commonwealth links after World War II have tended to bring both countries together in some respects. With the establishment of the Shastri Indo-Canadian Institute, scholarly interaction and exchange has increased considerably between India and Canada.

The similarities between Canada and the United States, as noted earlier, need not mislead us to consider both countries as the same without any distinctions whatsoever. In spite of an unguarded border between the two countries, Canadians have not only succeeded in maintaining a distinct political identity but also have become a part of a conservative value syndrome uncharacteristic of Americans.

Canadian society and polity have demonstrated an evolutionary pattern of development as opposed to a revolutionary pattern associated with American society (Preston 1979). Naegele (1968) and Lipset (1963) have pointed out that while Canada and the United States to a very great extent share the same values of achievement and egalitarianism, in Canada the emphasis is somewhat less and these values are held much more tentatively. In this context, as noted by Lipsett, the test of the utility of the comparative approach to the two North American societies so similar in value orientations depends upon specifying the special differences that do exist.

French-English linguistic dualism (Rocher, 1977: 484-493), ethnic pluralism (Porter, 1979: 89-162) - cultural mosaic ideal have been considered as important characteristics of Canadian society. This cultural diversity, prolonged dependency on the British, and perennial immigration and emmigration of people have contributed to the lack of a strong and distinct Canadian national identity. Moreover, Canadian society is more ascriptive, particularistic, collectively-oriented and elitist (Lipset) than the United States. The slow development of sociology in Canada can be attributed, in large part, to the traditional, conservative, and evolutionary nature of Canadian society itself.

II

The development of sociology in Canada[1] has been shaped by the unique characteristics of Canada as well as trends in sociology in the United States. The unique characteristics of Canada include the country's geography, mass immigration, frontier settlement after 1945, ties with Great Britain and the presence of a large minority linguistic and cultural group, the French Canadians. American sociology has been quite influential in Canada because, although many Canadian university departments are modelled after the British system, there were few precedents in sociology. For this reason, and because of proximity and similar social problems, Canadians turned to the United States for guidance (Elkin, 1958: 1102). Sociology in Canada, however, has not developed along one course, as "English Canadian" and "French Canadian" sociology have become two differentiated bodies of knowledge. The existence of two cultures within a single Canadian state has been paralleled to the development of two major streams of - French Canadian and English Canadian - sociology.

French Canadian sociology began at approximately the turn of the twentieth century with the rising concerns of the Catholic Church with social problems. Initially, Francophone sociology in Quebec was influenced by sociology in France. One of the earliest Quebec sociologists Leon Gerin had studied in Paris under LePlay's followers, and had adapted their systematic scheme for the analysis of society to describe rural communities, families, population, religion, parishes and land use.

The LePlay School was interested in the nature and problems of rural Quebec and sociologists were motivated by reformist zeal. The Catholic Church was, in major part, responsible for fostering this kind of sociological tradition. Prior to World War II, the LePlay school and the Catholic church action groups - both using the social action perspective were responding to the problems of change or lack of it in Quebec society.

In the preWorld War II period the Chicago School and in the post War period the Parsonian School have had some minor influence on French Canadian sociology. However, the relationship of French

Canadian sociology with European sociology, especially French sociology, has been quite significant.

As noted earlier, French Canadian sociology grew in a climate of service to the church and society. Therefore, many research interests were of an applied nature, such as problems of rural communities, urbanization, industrialization, and Quebec nationalism. Interestingly, departments of French Canadian sociology were not only often organized within philosophy departments, whereas English Canadian sociology was more frequently a part of economics departments.

French Canadian sociology tended to develop a more "holistic" approach and greater methodological awareness than the English Canadian sociology. The minority status of Francophones in Canada has influenced the content of French Canadian sociology. The applied nature of studying relevant issues is characteristic of French Canadian sociology. In recent decades, French Canadian sociologists have focussed their attention on issues such as labor management relations, Quebec nationalism-seperatism, stratification, and power and conflict by using holistic, Marxist and radical perspectives.

French Canadian sociology resembled European sociology in that theoretical, ideological and technical issues were dealt with much more than in English Canadian sociology. While the sociological explosion was occurring in the U.S., the growth of sociology in English Canada was hindered by the entrenchment in English-speaking universities of social history, which to some extent substituted for formal sociology; and the absence of salient social issues which would have stimulated and hastened the emergence of sociological enquiry (Forcese and Richer, 1975: 455-466).

In contrast, the relative ease with which sociology was incorporated into French-speaking universities is attributed to the social action programs of the catholic church and the consciousness of social problems and issues such as industrialization, urbanization, and changing social institutions and secularization process in Quebec. As we look back, this appears to be a good illustration of the interaction between social milieu and the development of sociology.

Sociology found a fertile ground in the American university system as it was free from rigid disciplinary boundaries and budget restraints. The university system in English Canada was not so flexible and open, since they were constrained by traditional British definitions of appropriate university based subjects. Moreover, social problems associated with urbanization and large-scale immigration found in the U.S. were relatively limited in Canada in that these problems were on a much smaller scale because of its vast, largely rural territory and scattered and limited population. In fact, Canada remained primarily a rural country until World War II and hence it did not face major problems of sociological interest as did the U.S. In this historical context, sociology developed more slowly in English Canada than in the U.S. and developed in somewhat different ways. Given the rural character of Canada, it has been observed (Forcese and Richer, 1975) that sociological inquiry in Canada focused on rural rather than urban communities and rendered incongruous both the Chicago and Parsonian schools imported into Anglophone Canada.

From the vantage point of the sociology of knowledge, (Rocher, 1977) it is noted that French Canada is an extremely interesting case for the study of the relationships between the practice of sociology and the values of a given society. When sociology, as a scientific discipline, made its first appearance in Quebec it encountered the resistance of the Catholic church. As an alternative, a sociology founded on what was called "sound Christian doctrine" was encouraged.

Rocher draws a clear distinction between the Francophone and the Anglophone parts of the discipline. In the Anglophone setting, it is more through their research that sociologists have provided leadership, whether for the benefit of governments, businesses or associations. In the Francophone setting, it is more through their global analysis and their participation in the "quiet revolution" in Quebec that sociologists have had an influence.

Furthermore, Canadian sociology reflects the Canadian duality of language and culture in that French and English Canadian sociologies[2], with a few exceptions, remain as 'two almost impermeable worlds' - 'two solitudes'. For Rocher, this cleavage between two worlds of language and thought confirms the "two nation theory" for Canada. In fact, very few Anglophone Canadian and American sociologists know anything of contemporary French sociology published in Quebec, France or elsewhere. But French-language sociology, as Rocher emphasized, cannot ignore English-language sociology to the same degree that the latter ignores French-language sociology, since the weight of the American sociological production is too overpowering to allow total isolation. Therefore, he makes a plea for increased communication among French and English- speaking sociologists and stresses the need for comparative research on common issues of social concern and action.

III

English Canadian sociology emerged under the influence of protestant religions, academic history, and the importation of the Chicago and Parsonian schools of sociology from the United States.

Those persons with theological backgrounds and who were trained to be on college or university faculties made early efforts in Anglophone Canada to introduce sociology as a course for formal instruction. Such efforts can be noted in the case of the Universities of Toronto (1914), McGill (1922), Manitoba (1910), British Columbia (1930s), Acadia (1908), Dalhousie (1927), St. Francis Xavier (1928), and Brandon College (1910), the United College (1911).

Studies in Canadian history, at least up until the late 1950s, appear to have provided sociological analysis. For instance, Harold Innis and Arthur Lower influenced the work of early Canadian sociologists such as S. D. Clark. It should also be pointed out that at the University of Toronto sociology under the banner of the department of political economy was for a long time dominated by history, economics, and political studies. So, sociology could develop neither a separate department nor a distinctive approach. Robert MacIver who taught at the University of Toronto (1911-1927) before he moved to Columbia University was unable to introduce a sociology program at Toronto. A separate department of sociology at the University of Toronto under the leadership of S. D. Clark[3] did not come into existence until the 1960s.

The first department of sociology in Canada was founded in 1922 at McGill University by C.A. Dawson. He was trained at the University of Chicago, and he emphasized empirical research in the tradition of the Chicago School of sociology. Dawson initiated a series of community studies and received what was at athe time a huge sum of $100,000 as a research grant from the Rockefeller Foundation, for the study of unemploymnet and ethnic background. Later on (1927) Everett Hughes also a Chicago-trained sociologist joined McGill's department of sociology and published the now classic "French Canada in Transition".

Until the 1960s McGill and Toronto were perhaps the only two major sociology departments among Canadian universities. While the former was under the influence of the Chicago school, the latter was under the influence of structural-functional school, especially when Dennis Wrong and S. M. Lipset taught in the Parsonian tradition there. The two dominant traditions of American sociology therefore made their impact on sociology teaching and research in Canada through these two founding schools.

English Canadian Sociology has taken a less integrated and encompassing approach to studying society than its French counterpart. As a result, the whole effort generally has not been very concerned with theoretical and methodological aspects; nor was much work been done on the ideological role of sociologists. Rather, sociologists appear to have been most concerned with making up for the lack of information about Canadian society instead of seeking to adopt some holistic perspective (Conner and Curtis, 1970: 33). Thus, a realistic and holistic picture of the evolution of Canadian society and its future has not been forthcoming. Instead what has emerged is "an abstract, bland, fragmental and static picture of Canadian society" (Davis, 1970: 32). This characteristic of English Canadian sociology has been explained as the result of the pre-occupation with structural functionalism imported from the United States.

Canadian sociology in general has suffered from the problems associated with inadequate funding, such as heavy teaching loads, a lack of research assistants and a lack of money specifically designated for research. As well, other problems arose from a weak public image of the social sciences and a structurally weak institutional framework have hindered the progress of sociology. For example the Canadian Sociology and Anthropology Association was not established until 1965. Partly as a result of these factors Canadian sociology has made little impact internationally, and many of the best professionals and graduate students have been lost to American universities and universities abroad.

Canadian sociology did not begin to expand until the late 1950s. Through the 1960s, sociology as an academic discipline expanded rapidly in Canada because of high university enrollments in general, and particularly in sociology courses. In the 1970s, because of a growing demand for its distinctive Canadian orientation to problems of society, there was considerable introspection by Canadian sociologists about the state of the discipline and profession. However, during the 1960s - a period of great expansion, there were not enough Canadians to fill teaching positions. Thus, many Americans had to be imported. Even as late as in 1970-71, only 40.3% of all sociologists and anthropologists in Canada were Canadian citizens while 38.5% were American (Rotstein and Lax, 1974:199).

The fact that only thirteen doctoral degrees were granted in Canada from 1955 to 1969 obviously necessitated the importation of a large number of American-trained sociologists because of rapid expansion of sociology departments in Canadian universities resulting from the post-war demographic changes and affluence. The professional socialization, experiences of sociologists in the U.S. (Lambert and Curtis, 1973) who have been teaching in large numbers in Canadian universities tended to influence the nature of sociology in Canada. Even graduate students in Canada followed the American model.

The presence of these American scholars in Canadian universities no doubt affected the direction and character of Canadian sociology (Beattie and Crysdale, 1974). Similarly, the lack of adequate graduate schools in sociology in Canada, compared to the large number of American departments, meant that more American influences were brought in with returning students. It is possibly because of this dependency on American universities for training and faculty members, that Canadian sociology during the 1960s, neither contributed extensively to the development of national consciousness nor to the study of high priority problems in Canadian society. Likewise, sociologists in Canada generally did not participate in the general intellectual and political life of the nation, possibly because they were more oriented towards American society, and the American academic community.

It is only since the early 1970s that a gradual trend toward Canadianization of sociology has been noticed. In fact, in recent years there seems to be tough competition among Canadian graduates for faculty positions in sociology departments. Since the mid 1970s, the growing unemployment among Canadian graduates, along with strict immigration policies, appears to have considerably reduced the influx of American sociologists.

A study conducted in the late 1960s (Connor and Curtis, 1970) reported that a large minority of sociologists in Canada expressed their interest and specialization in areas such as: social organization and institutions, social change, social problems, population, community studies, and social psychology. The Chicago ecological school was seen to have had a major impact on Canadian sociology. This study argued that a large backlog of descriptive work should be carried out as a basis for later more theoretical work, and as a necessary input into the development of more effective social policy.

Furthermore, Connor and Curtis recognized that a great deal of the research carried out up to the late 1960s was of an adhoc character. Holistic and integrated approaches were infrequent, especially in English Canadian sociology. The differences between the sociology in English and French Canadian sociologies were not only discernable but also seemed to be well established.

In the late 1960s, a large majority of sociologists had research projects underway and used such methods of research as interview schedules, questionnaire, library research, and computer data processing. The research role of sociologists was increasingly challenged by the rising demands of teaching responsibilities, administrative duties, and the competition for scarce funds. The common complaints then were the lack of trained research assistants, lack of funding agencies, lack of funds, especially absence of long term funds, shortage of research facilities etc. In recent years, the research facilities and funding in universities have improved considerably.

Sociology and social and cultural anthropology in Canada seem to be closely linked. For instance, there is one major professional association for sociologists and anthropologists. Also, it was found (Connor and Curtis, 1970) that despite distinct disciplinary backgrounds there was often an overlap of interests. Some anthropologists listed sociological topics as their first professional interest while conversely some sociologists listed anthropological topics. In recent years, however, there has been considerable differentiation and specialization between sociologists and social-cultural anthropologists in terms of research areas, approaches and emphases.

As far as professional sociological organizations and publications were concerned Canada, is a latecomer compared to India. While the **Indian Sociological Society** came into existence and published its official journal in 1951, it was not until 1964 that the **Canadian Sociology and Anthropology Association** and its Journal appeared. The **Canadian Review of Sociology and Anthropology** has been serving as a communication link for both the sociologists and anthropologists of English and French Canada.

The **Canadian Journal of Sociology** made its first appearance in 1975. Since then it has provided an additional outlet for sociologists to publish their researches. In addition, French Canadian sociologists have their own professional organization, and journals which devote greater attention to Quebec society and its problems. A content analysis (Anderson, et al., 1975) of journal articles revealed the predominance of the areas such as stratification, religion, community studies, and social problems. The late growth of sociology in Canadian universities shown by the fact that there were only ten sociologists in 1938, 69 in 1955-56 and then about 600 in 1973, explains the late emergence of professional organizations and journals in Canada.

The plenary session on the "Future of Sociology in Canada" held in 1970 in Winnipeg discussed some important issues[4] confronting the discipline and the profession. Questions were raised regarding the role of values in sociology, manpower problems and the training of sociologists -- especially the domination by American sociologists and American sociology in English Canada, the teaching of sociology with reference to Canadian content of courses, research resources, and professional concerns of French and English Canadian sociologists.

Coburn (1970: 37-51) noted that the history of sociology in Canada had been one of under-development and neglect because of the education of Canadians abroad, and importation of foreign scholars who lack knowledge of the Canadian scene. He mentioned a number of areas of weakness in Canadian sociology, such as: the failure of sociologists to take into account the high priority problems of their own society, a lack of participation in the general intellectual and political life of the nation, the under development of graduate education and of research, and the problems posed by the low population of Canadian scholars in Sociology.

Davis (1970: 30-35) focused on some failings of Anglophone sociology in Canada and advanced the thesis that, by and large, it has 'failed to present a realistic and holistic picture of the evolution of Canadian society'. Sociologists in English Canada, seeing through a middle class lens, have presented an 'abstract, bland, fragmented and static picture of Canadian society'. The reasons for the aridity of Anglophone sociology in Canada were attributed to the preoccupation with structural-functionalism[5] and the general identification of middle class anglophone sociologists with the Anglo- Canadian bourgeois Establishment - a branch plant of the American capitalist empire. He advocated that the traditional mainstream sociology in Canada (and the U.S.) should therefore be supplemented by a dialectical perspective.

IV

Indian and Canadian sociologies have some similarities because of their similar histories, being British colonies at one time. However, there have also been historical differences. Canadian sociology was more influenced by American and European schools than by British sociology, in contrast to Indian sociology which was heavily influenced by British sociology and anthropology, at least up till 1947. Although Canadian sociology did not acquire a close relationship with anthropology from the British, this association nevertheless, developed. Many of the similarities which shall be pointed out between Indian and Canadian sociology appear to be the result of being intellectually dependent on foreign schools of sociology.

Both Canadian and Indian sociology have experienced the influence of American sociology - its emphasis on empiricism. This empiricism has been especially adopted by English Canadian sociologists, who have accepted it with little or no questioning and give the impression of never having developed any philosophical background or questioned any of the assumptions. Indian sociologists have also adopted American empiricism, although much questioning has taken place and the unique Indian historical, philosophical background has been derived and emphasized. The Indian philosophical background, which has been gleaned from Hinduism, provided an encompassing view of social life, allowing sociologists to assume a more encompassing and integrative approach. Similarly, French Canadian sociology has sought to develop such holistic approaches.

Both national schools of sociology have had a trend marked by the predominance of descriptive studies. This had led to the lack of theoretical development in both Indian and Canadian sociologists. The descriptive studies are necessary, however, in that in both countries there is a backlog of information which must be collected before theories can be formulated and problematic social issues can be examined. In both countries there seems to be a growing awareness that sociology must seek to become more active in public affairs by making research findings of relevance to decision-makers and possibly taking a stand on issues.

Canadian sociology, as stated earlier, during the 1950s and 1960s, has suffered from a similar lack of resources that has affected Indian sociology, through heavy teaching loads, lack of money for research and inadequate graduate schools. This has meant the loss of many teachers, researchers and students to foreign countries. In both countries, sociology suffers from being structurally weak in institutional organization although steps are being taken to alleviate this problem. If Canadian sociology contains two major streams, i.e. English and French Canadian sociologies, Indian sociology, in recent years, has shown signs of the emergence of regional sociologies in various regional languages.

While both Canadian and Indian sociology have grown up under the wings of foreign schools of sociology it appears that the Indians have reacted most strongly to this domination, while Canadians have been more placid, before the 1970s. The Indian reaction has involved the past, the reaffirmation of the importance of Indian philosophies of life for understanding society. In contrast, no such distinctive frame of reference was emphasized in Canada until recently. Although reactions against foreign domination have been especially felt in the realm of staffing universities, now that there are more Canadian graduates in sociology, a stress on the need for a distinct Canadian sociology has begun to emerge. Sociology has not yet reached that stage of academic maturity present in American sociology in either country and still appears to be undergoing much soul-searching.

V

We have noted the influence of American sociology on the early development of sociology in English Canada. This influence has continued with great vigor after World War II, because of several forces within Canada and its close proximity to America, and the economic, political and cultural domination of the U.S. The process of globalization of American sociology is felt nowhere more than in Canada. S. D. Clark (1975: 225) succinctly[6] states, 'what has developed here is not a Canadian sociology but a sociology that is American'.

It is recognized (Lambert and Curtis, 1973: 76-78) that the presence of a large majority of American sociologists in Canadian universities seriously hampered the growth and development of a Canadian sociology. Furthermore, Canadian sociology (Stolzman and

Gamberg, 1975) cannot be built up by adopting putatively universal models whose utilization is tantamount to filling American theoretical categories with Canadian information. In the 1970s some Canadian sociologists began to feel that prevailing paradigms, theories and research in American sociology were irrelevant or inapplicable to Canadian society.

Canadian society, as we noted earlier, is different in some respect from the United States. In Canada there seems to be a chasm between French and English speaking populations in general, and sociologists in particular. French Canadian sociologists are primarily concerned with Quebec society just as American sociologists are concerned with the problems of their society. But Anglophone sociologists in Canada until recently tended to view sociology as a discipline seeking universal principles of social interaction and society, and so hardly made deliberate attempts to develop a national sociology with its own models to explain Canadian reality.

During the early 1970s, however, several sociologists in Canada realized that a Canadian sociology, with its own communication network, research interests, and ideological commitments, might lead to the emergence of theories and models which differ from those of American sociology. Since the 1960s there have been a substantial number of sociological studies - monographs, Canadian texts and anthologies, articles, reports etc. - about Canadian society, and these have been on the increase in recent years. Despite the proliferation of Canadian sociological literature, it is pointed out that the only thing that all these studies have in common is that they are concerned with subjects that have something to do with Canada, they lack a sociological approach that is unique to Canadian social reality.

Despite the benefits that may be derived from international linkages, it is recognized that Canadian society furnishes a natural laboratory for distinctive Canadian investigations of a variety of problems. Keyfitz (1974) remarks that Canada has rarely developed identifiable 'schools of thought' and few, if any, Canadian social scientists are seen as pioneers in the theoretical development of their subjects because the approach characteristic of Canadian social science has been eclectic and pragmatic rather than philosophical. This issue demands further examination.

It is believed that though the problems for sociological research in Canada and the U.S.A. seem to be similar there are problems of national concern which are unique to each country. Moreover, one cannot overlook the fact that the U.S. is so big, in both intellectual and material output, that it necessarily imposes its theories, methods and its subjects on sociology in Canada and elsewhere. Despite this dominant influence of American sociology, it is important to note that sociologies in India, Britain, Japan, Germany, Africa, France, Scandinavia, Latin America have their own distinctive characteristics as well.

The slow process of institutionalization of sociology in Canada coupled with lack of national identity provide some explanation for the late emergence of a Canadian sociology movement. Keyfitz demonstrated that there is a potential Canadian sociology capable of inspiring creative research in areas such as Canadian nationalism - identity, biculturalism, resources, education, and foreign aid. He urged sociologists to develop Canadian sociology with a specific focus on these issues.

VI
During the 1970s some Canadian sociologists (Clark, 1973: Stolzman and Gamberg, 1975: Lambert and Curtis, 1973; Davis, 1970) criticized American sociologists and American sociology for undermining the development of Canadian sociology. During 1950-70 a large majority of American sociologists in Canadian universities disseminated a brand of sociology that is American. Canadian sociology assumed a distinctly American flavor, frequently with American interpretation of Canadian problems.

In a paradigmatic sense it was argued (Watson, 1975: 345) that this situation provided an excellent example of the crucial interlacing of economic power and ideational power. This paradigm is considered to be valid in view of the fact of America's global hegemony in contemporary sociology and Canada's historical colonial relationship to the United States.

The assumption underlying the need for a Canadian sociology with its own theoretical concepts and orientations is that Canadian society is not only different from but also unique in many respects in relation to the United States. The use of American sociological models provided by Park and Parsons, for instance, in studying Canadian society and its problems are considered not relevant for understanding distinct cultural diversities in Canada. Even the recent radical-Neo-Marxian sociology that has surfaced in Canada is considered to be an importation from the United States, with little or no meaning in terms of the Canadian experience.

In the context of sociology conceived as a science seeking for universal principles of human relationships, the necessity for a distinctly Canadian theoretical orientation is not considered absurd. The effort to Canadianize the discipline calls for a thoroughgoing intellectual revolt against the imported models of American sociology.

Canada, it is claimed, suffers from an American economic, political, and cultural hegemony which undermines Canada's sovereignty. There is therefore, a need for a Canadian sociology to study not only the factors that have contributed to the survival of the nation but also those forces leading to the economic, political, and cultural domination by the United States. The stress on a distinct Canadian sociology is thus intertwined with the dreams of and aspirations for a truly independent Canadian nation.

These Canadian nationalistic sentiments among some Canadian sociologists incorporate the notion that American sociology harbors an imperialistic bias behind a facade of universality, and that the application of American sociology to the study of Canadian society directly or indirectly buttresses American hegemony over Canada. Therefore, in the process of developing a national sociology it is necessary to reject those models taken from American sociology to observe the nature of Canadian social reality.

It is believed that the functionalism and abstracted empiricism which charactertize mainstream American sociology have adverse effects on Canadian sociology. For instance, functionalism has favoured continentalism, creating false consciousness among Canadians as a nation which must depend on the United States for economic, military, and cultural support. Abstracted empiricism has contributed to several studies on trivial, unimportant problems, while neglecting topics that are controversial and of national importance. Moreover, American sociology primarily upholds the interests of the dominant groups and overlooks the disadvantaged groups.

It is therefore stated (Stolzman and Gamberg, 1975: 103) that 'the mere accumulation of Canadian data channelled into unexamined American theoretical boxes may bring about an increase in the volume of sociological literature on discrete Canadian topics, but it cannot be the basis for the creation of a genuine Canadian sociology.' The key precondition to a truly national sociology, it is argued, lies in Canadians undergoing a process of hightened national awareness which can stimulate in Canadian sociology the necessary vigilance about pseudo- universal American models of sociology.

Thus, the emergence of Canadian nationalism and a call for the development of a relevant Canadian[7] sociology are responses to cultural, political, economic domination of Canadian society by the United States. The need for a relevant Anglo-Canadian sociology, as noted earlier, has also arisen partly as a reaction to the declining or stabilizing university enrollments and the fear of unemployment for younger Canadian sociologists.

VII

What is Canadian sociology? There are different conceptions

of Canadian sociology. The labour market conception of Canadian sociology is sociology done by Canadians, i.e. citizens, graduates of Canadian universities, and permanent residents. In this sense Canadian sociology is perceived in terms of those actors who indulge in sociology teaching and research who have Canadian nationality. Canadian course content and research are supposed to be interlinked.

There is also a belief that sociological research on Canadian society requires a sensitive knowledge of the society which can be best undertaken by Canadians rather than by non-Canadians. So, it is presumed that hiring more Canadians and providing more Canadian content in sociology courses may contribute to the development of Canadian sociology, but there is no guarantee that it will lead to a distinctly Canadian theoretical orientation.

Those who advocate a specifically Canadian theoretical approach tend to adopt a sociology of knowledge perspective in that sociological paradigms are derived from the experiences of nations within specific time periods. Clement (1977) makes a distinction between a 'sociology of Canada and Canadian sociology'. The former is restricted to the level of 'macro groupings' at best, and at a micro sociological level at worst. The latter attempts to move between the analytical levels of national and total societies. It is asserted that a macro-sociological political economy perspective would be appropriate to develop a Canadian sociology - a Canadian paradigm grounded in the Canadian experience. In other words, it is argued that a national sociology with unique theoretical concepts and frameworks is necessary and possible.

Canadian sociology, it is suggested (Felt, 1975: 382), can also be derived from an eclectic, social problems orientation to Canadian society. To be relevant is to work for the improvement of society and to engage in social praxis. There seems to be uncertainty, though, as to the possibility and feasibility of a national (i.e. Canadian) praxis, given the present state of the discipline. In the context of nationalist feelings, the preference is for the development of a number of paradigms within Canadian sociology. Others (Gurstein, 1972: Stolzman and Gamberg, 1975; Clement, 1977) maintain that a contextualized Canadian sociology theoretically appropriate to Canadian society and its problems is desirable and possible. It is believed (Hofley, 1981: 602) though, that there are some fundamental 'tensions' in the works of most, if not all, sociologists in Canada today, which affect the development of a theory of Canadian society.

Canadian sociology has been criticized for its failure to recognize the historical, philosophical and epistomological underpinnings of the discipline which are frequently sacrificed on the altar of positivism. It is claimed to be obsessed with methodological purism, "mindless militant empiricism" (Walsh, 1972) and to lack a viable intellectual left. Moreover, the impoverished nature of Canadian sociology cannot be solely attributed to 'the American take-over. Canadian sociology is not deemed to have succeeded in developing its own models for analysing the unique Canadian social reality.

Furthermore, as Watson (1975: 354-62) points out, Anglophone Canadian sociology, with very few exceptions, has not engaged in a systematic critique of the political economy, the service institutions, and structural inequality. In other words, Anglophone Canadian sociologists, for the most part, have not presented a radical critical analysis of their society. So, the poverty of Anglophone Canadian sociology lies in its failure to appreciate the need for structural analysis which seek to explore the 'domain assumptions' of social arrangements, and the need to critically evaluate the dominant ideology of Canadian society.

The theoretical dearth of Canadian sociology is quite obvious considering a proliferation of micro-quantitative studies, which by themselves hardly contribute to a science of society. The preoccupation of mainstream Anglophone Canadian sociology with 'abstracted empiricism' scientific objectivity, and methodological rigor has kept most sociologists from examining the values implicit in their enterprise. Margrit Eichler and Patricia Marchak (1985), among others, have focused atention on the issue of value free sociology in Canada.

Most Anglophone Canadian sociologists, however, have failed to ask questions about their traditional social institutions, and seem to have accepted the status quo by default. Francophone Canadian sociologists have been more structurally informed and critical about Quebec and Canada with far reaching implications for change of social systems.

From the perspective of theory it has been argued (Watson, 1975) that some of the poverty of Canadian sociology could be alleviated through the structural critique of the Canadian political economy, by demystifying the reified aspects of society such as class conflict, exploitation, racism, power relations, and coercive social control. Methodologically, it is stated that the adoption of participant observation, coupled with the interpretation of what is observed in terms of the purposes and of the culture observed would be useful for explaining change.

It is further maintained (Watson, 1975: 359) that 'only by deliberately rejuvenating theoretical perspectives on Canadian society will we be able to move away from the current orientation to the nitpicking, narrowly empirical shallow waters of sociology, to the deep substream of social reality, in all its intersubjective and spontaneous diversity'.

The same approach and emphasis can be found in Clement's (1977) advocacy of a Canadian sociology which is consistent with the task of theory construction. According to him, Canadian sociology is the application of classical approaches used by Marx and Weber to macro-sociological issues of Canadian society. It is within the tradition of holistic analysis that he calls for a reflexive relationship between theory and research and the redevelopment of sociologies at several levels of analysis, especially as they relate to one another, including an understanding of the past, present and an eye to the future.

VIII

Hiller (1979: 125-145) demonstrates how the 'Canadianization' issue within the discipline of sociology in Canada has resulted in an identifiable 'Canadian sociology movement'. The initial emphasis of the movement,[8] as we discussed earlier, was primarily on personnel matters i.e. hiring policies. During this first phase, there was a major focus on sociologists' Canadian nationality, identity, training, ideology, research issues, and theory critical of mainline sociological theories. During the second phase, the movement stresses perspective and content. In this stage the emphasis is subject matter. The sociologist is expected to ask questions raised by the study of Canadian society itself, and, by using research methods that are appropriate to the issue, develop theoretical frameworks from Canadian data, thereby contributing to the Canadian sociological perspective and literature. In this context, national issues and the national milieu become relevant and important.

It is evident that sociology in Canada has depended more heavily than sociology in India on American sociology, not only for theoretical approaches and methodologies but also for personnel, texts, and professional organizations. In recent years there has been some change with regard to the latter three areas. Preference is being given to Canadian and Canadian trained sociologists by an increasing number of sociology departments. Canadian texts, readers, monograph series, and journals have gradually increased. Graduate and undergraduate courses have been becoming more Canadian in content and relevance (Lamy, 1976). However, there is still a long way to go in the direction of Canadianization[9] of sociology training and practice.

Many of the sociological studies on Canadian society are said to be primarily empirical in nature, without a distinct theoretical approach that is unique to Canadian social reality. The Canadian sociology movement, which is still in its second phase, has been struggling hard to differentiate Canadian sociology from American sociology. A Canadian sociology[10] with its unique theoretical perspective and or methodological emphasis, if any, has yet to emerge.

For Hiller, 'if the movement is to be more than merely an exercise in consciousness-raising, the Canadian sociological perspective(s) must continue to coagulate so that it can be one of the critical funnels into which data is organized to make sociology in Canada both societally relevant and internationally strong'.

IX

Compared to the 1950s, in the 1980s the number and size of departments of sociology have increased. Today there are more than 45 universities and colleges across Canada that have introduced sociology. Despite stabilizing and declining enrollments, the demand for sociology has not substantially diminished. In Quebec, Francophone sociology is dominated by the universities of Laval and Montreal. In the case of Anglophone universities the pre-eminent status of the universities of Toronto and McGill is being challenged by universities such as Carleton, York, McMaster, Calgary, Alberta, British Columbia and Waterloo, through their graduate programs, and research and publication activities.

The financial support for sociological research from the SSHRC (Social Science and Humanities Research Council) increased quite considerably during the 1970s through doctoral and post-doctoral research grants. In the 1980s there has been an emphasis on not only individual but also team and interdisciplinary research into topics considered to be priority areas, such as Aging, Family and Socialization, Technology etc.[11] This quantitative increase in sociology in Canada has important implications for the nature and growth of Canadian sociology.

Despite this quantitative increase, Anglophone Canadian sociology in particular has not yet been able to clearly distinguish itself from American sociology. Furthermore, it seems to be still heavily dependent on American sociology for theories, methods and intellectual stimulation, probably because of cultural similarity and lack of a strong national identity.[12] In contrast, Francophone Canadian sociology is less dependent on American sociology because of differences in language and culture and strong national aspirations. French Canadian sociology manifests an identifiable distinct tradition as opposed to Anglophone sociology.

This is not to say, however, that Anglophone Canadian sociology has not shown any signs of developing new and distinct trends. As a matter of fact, Hiller (1981: 1297-1307) while discussing the social context of Canadian publishing shows how national forces, relevance, and ethnocentrism influence sociological work in Anglophone Canada. An examination of

Anglophone books published in Canada primarily during 1978-80 demonstrated that many Canadian sociologists are now engaged in issues that pertain to Canadian society, or have implications for the national society. The major themes of these books focus upon power and inequality, and ethnicity, deviance, the family, and a wide range of substantive areas.

This preoccupation with Canadian issues of identity, unity, and survival by sociologists in Canada, and the 'Canadianization' of Canadian publishing is considered to be a response to the felt need to understand more fully the contours and dynamics of Canadian society. This 'micro' research followed by 'macro' analysis may lead to new and creative insights. But as far as Canadian sociology introductory texts[13] are concerned, Hiller (1981: 1305) states that 'What began as a Canadian rejection of American texts for their national orientation and apparent ethnocentrism, has resulted in Canadian texts with at least as equally strong **Canadian** orientation and even perhaps greater ethnocentrism.'

Clement (1977) argues, however, that the focus of a Canadian sociology should be on an array of substantive problems in Canadian society.[14] These problems in turn must be worked out in terms of the priorities of each researcher, which implies an evaluation of what are considered important or significant social issues and concerns. Is there a uniqueness to Canadian society that makes it a valuable topic beyond its intrinsic interest to its residents? After having answered in the affirmative, Clement advocates the adoption of the political economy tradition, for developing Canadian sociology, as the most fruitful approach, because of its strong historical roots which can provide the greatest insights into Canada's social structure.

The evidence presented so far demonstrates that the institutionalization of sociology as a discipline and profession in Canada has been influenced by the socio-cultural milieu characteristic of Canada. More importantly, American sociology has for long dominated Anglophone sociology in Canada. It was only during the 1970s that Canadian sociologists became more vociferous in raising questions as to the relevance of American sociology for Canada.

A group of Canadian sociologists, as we noted earlier, have reacted against American academic imperialism by calling for a sociology that is unique to Canada. For some sociologists, at least, this implies a Canadian sociology with its own theoretical perspectives and models in order to understand and explain Canadian realities. Questioning by Canadian sociologists about the relevance of American sociology to Canadian society appears to be intertwined with the aspirations of a strong Canadian national sovereignty. In fact, a Canadian sociologist (Crook, 1975: 497) states that the 'problem of a distinct English Canadian sociology is precisely an expression of the problem of Canadian nationhood itself'.

National sentiments are so strong that the social sciences, and sociology in particular, are considered by some nationalists as hotbeds of American orientations and models, and the hiring of non-Canadians for university positions is strongly resisted. In such a situation, coupled with increasing proportion of sociologists trained in Canada looking for jobs, sociology plays a complex and delicate part in gaining an understanding of the complex fabric of Canadian society.

On the one hand it is recognized that it is useful to view Canada in comparative terms but it is not considered appropriate to uncritically import American theory and data unmindful of their relevance and applicability to the Canadian society, on the other. Moreover, since most American sociology has not been comparative in its conceptualization, theoretical orientations and research, it is considered fruitless for social action in Canada. The underlying assumption seems to be that sociology is a form of goal-oriented social and political activity.

The Canadian sociology movement which has emerged in recent years, apart from its emphasis on the Canadianization of personnel, curriculum and texts, has also stressed the need for macro historical comparative research on Canadian issues and problems by using political economy perspective (Marchak, 1985). This again focuses not on status quo but on action-change in Canadian society. Thus, a beginning has been made in this direction. Besides structuralism (Richardson R.J. and B. Wellman, 1985), and phenomenology (O'Neill, 1985), Canadian Sociology has been influenced by feminist (Eichler, 1985) and critical (Morrow, 1985) approaches. However, there is still a long way to go for Canadian sociology to achieve unique theoretical orientations and research traditions..

Thus, sociology in both India and Canada has been shaped not only by their respective socio-cultural milieu but also by the influence of American sociology. The differential impact of American sociology on India and Canada is quite evident in the differing patterns of growth of sociology in these two countries.

The foregoing delineation of sociology in the United States, India, and Canada sets the stage for a comparative analysis of the role of sociologists, and the values and goals of sociology across nations. In the next chapter, we shall examine the nature of consensus and controversy that prevails in these rather crucial aspects of the discipline and profession of sociology.

CHAPTER 6

CONSENSUS AND CONTROVERSY:
ROLES OF SOCIOLOGISTS AND
VALUES-OBJECTIVITY DILEMMA

I

Values form a significant part of the images and roles of sociologists.[1] Sociologists have been stereotyped in terms of various kinds of images. The sociologist has been viewed (Berger, P., 1963) as a secularized version of the liberal protestant ministry, as a theoretician for social work, as a social reformer, as a gatherer of statistics of human behavior, as a cold manipulator of people, as a professional peeping Tom, or as an intellectual who is half humanist and half scientist. Let us not examine in detail those images at this point. Our primary concern is to discuss the roles of sociologists as teachers, researchers, and practitioners.

The principal image that sociologists project, according to Lee (1978: 70), is that of value-free scientists wedded to esoteric terminology, to impressive quantification, to statistical manipulation, and to theories of human relations and social structure based on what is claimed to be "hard data".

Despite this principal image, projected by a majority of sociologists, in every country disputes over the definition of the role of the sociologist persist.[2] Controversies over the allocation of the intellectual resources of sociologists are often put forward as conflicts of sociological ideas. However, there is consensus among sociologists as to their primary roles as teachers, researchers, and consultants.

An overwhelming majority of sociologists around the word assume the role of transmitters and producers of sociological knowledge in college and university settings.[3] This role is defined and perceived differently by sociologists and non-sociologists alike. One view associated with positivism is that sociologists are expected to be disinterested observers of social phenomena and are supposed to provide empirical data and objective analysis pertaining to social institutions, processes and problems of society. Sociologists, at the most, can play the role of academic critics, based on scientific knowledge.

Another view recognizes the role of sociologists as social engineer, applied sociologist, consultant, planner i.e. that of the professional. In the last few decades sociologists in the U.S.A. (Janowitz, 1972) have been increasingly assuming the role of the professional outside of academia.[4] In Canada, India and in other countries the applied sociologist still appears to be a rare species.

A third view based on radical humanism believes that sociologists by virtue of their specialized knowledge (social praxis) should play the role of activists and advocates for the improvement of society actively engaged in combating poverty, exploitation, racism, sexism, colonialism and so on.

It should be noted that not all roles involve the same degrees of commitment or constraint on the sociologists playing them. In fact, many sociologists, because of their training and values, have assumed one role; for instance that of disinterested-observer-scientist as opposed to applied sociologists or activist-advocate.

Of course, novelty and creativity in behavior is expected and at times demanded in many roles. The role of sociologist is no exception. However, a number of sociologists and different groups of people in society seem to have different expectations regarding the role of sociologists. Moreover, not all role expectations are regarded as equally legitimate. The development of the multiple roles of the sociologist is a recent phenomenon accelerated by increasing demands for the application of sociological knowledge to the solution of social problems and the improvement of societies.[5] In this context, the sociologist as consultant assumes unprecedented responsibility.

Despite critics' questioning of whether or not sociology truly can address itself to the improvement of the human condition, applied sociologists using different models - social engineering, radical sociology, enlightenment - may not provide definitive answers on which policy and professional practice may be based (Street and Weinstein, 1975; Janowitz, 1970); but applied sociology, it is claimed, can lead to more humane and effective decisions and better social institutions.

II

When considering the roles of sociologists, inevitably ethical and moral values and norms enter into the picture. In addition, the issue of scientific objectivity - value neutrality vs. value commitment is faced by every sociologist and usually resolved or compromised in a manner which is based on one's training, personal values, and institutional affiliation.

As far as the responsibility of social scientists is concerned, Markovic (1972) advocated that they must change their fundamental assumptions about the nature of their task, and replace previously dominant ideas of positive science and its methodology. Their traditional detachment and aloofness must give way to a very serious concern about all misuses of scientific findings for non-humane purposes. In fact, the very concept of value-free scientific social inquiry is said to be misleading because certain values and norms are always present in any social research.

Cognitive and non-cognitive values are invariably implicit in the theoretical and methodological pre-suppositions of social scientists. For example, sociologists using structural-functional theoretical perspective, by insisting on stability, harmony and order as prerequisites for the maintenance and continuity of social systems, try to defend the status quo. In contrast, sociologists with a Marxist orientation do not recognize the claims to legitimacy of that value system.

In this context, sociologists have different options open to them: a) They may pursue objective scientific research ignoring or subordinating ethical and moral values, socio-economic, political and cultural aspirations. b) They may defend the dominant ideology in a given society and time and help maintain the status quo. c) They may engage in a critical study from a universal humanist point of view. d) They may involve themselves as advocates and change agents aiming at change in the system or change of the system for human emancipation.

It is asserted (Glass, 1978) that the humane and the critical go together. For instance, critical theorists have rejected any positive theory building as they perceive all positive theories to have a system supporting function. So the purpose of a dialectical and social theory can only be criticism of a social reality and scientific theories. Those sociologists with a humanistic point of view tend to be directly involved in social practice. Humanistic sociologists are also concerned about the abuse of knowledge and are concerned about its practical applications.

Sociologists in their role as teachers have assumed paramount importance in view of the fact that more than 70% of sociologists are employed in colleges and universities for the primary purpose of teaching. In this role sociologists are expected not only to convey information and pass on accumulated sociological knowledge and skills but engage in the creative interpretation of knowledge by putting pieces of data into broader contexts, showing the interconnections and conditions under which knowledge was created and the implications for sociological research and practice. Sociologists as teachers are supposed to awaken the intellectual curiosity, broaden the horizon of students, and develop their capacities for critical thinking. The importance of oral transmission of sociological knowledge and the emergence of new ideas in this process, is well demonstrated (Merton R. K. and, M. W. Riley, 1980).

Sociologists belong to a nation, a socio-economic group, an ideology, a set of cultural traditions and are influenced by socialization process (graduate training), recent and contemporary events. The roles of sociologists as teachers, researchers, or practitioners are not free from these inevitable socio-cultural forces. Hence, it is difficult to overcome this limited intellectual horizon and to realize the ideal that sociology is a universal discipline. Sociologists as teachers are themselves culture-bound, and with few exceptions fail to socialize the next generation of sociologists to accept sociological perspectives that transcend national boundaries.

Sociologists have reflected on the nature of relationships between teachers and students and have developed a set of rules of ethics regulating such relationships. As far as student-teacher relations are concerned, a code of ethics for sociologists in India (1967) states that teachers should neither patronize nor hold prejudices against students on the basis of personal, ideological or communal considerations, and they should always provide opportunities for students to have freedom of thought. The code of ethics for American sociologists (1982) makes reference to the obligation of sociologists to protect the rights of students to fair treatment; and to refrain from coercing or exploiting students by virtue of their professional positions. A code of professional ethics for Canadian sociologists (1979) assigns the responsibility to train students to conduct themselves professionally before they carry out research, and states that the relationship of sociologists to students should be a non-exploitative one. These ethical codes for teachers of sociology rarely deal with the problems, if any, of ideological indoctrination in the classroom.

In India (Saran 1958: 1030-31) the role of the social scientist is very differently conceived now - as a social engineer rather than a theoretician. This is because of the government of India's commitment to planning-development-change, which has given a new turn to sociological research. Social research is increasingly becoming a huge monetary proposition financed by the government, thereby affecting the freedom of the sociologist in terms of the choice of areas and themes of research. It is feared that fundamental theoretical research and thinking will suffer, adversely affecting the quality of applied and empirical research as well. Despite the increasing recognition of the role of sociologists in national development, India is still far away from the kind of large scale use of sociologists in government and industry that exists in the United States.

The Indian Sociological Conference (1976) favoured the role of observer-analyst to the exclusion of the interventionist role for sociologists, and contended that the sociologist qua sociologist has neither the equipment nor the conviction for the interventionist role, though as individuals both ideological convictions and activism toward their materialization were in order. Sociologists were advised 'not to burn their fingers' by accepting technician's secondary roles, assigned by policy makers.

The counterview supporting the interventionist role was based on an empirical and epistemological inseperability of the three roles for social scientists. It was argued that an evaluation of the social reality went hand in hand with its observation and analysis, and consequently intervention in favour of the approved values was inevitable. Furthermore, sociologists could not absolve themselves of responsibility for their own findings.

The need for the sociologist's involvement in social policy formulation in India is still largely unmet, and the actual involvement of the sociologist in planning is still marginal. According to Gore (1984), the sociologist in India can play many different roles in the promotion of a social policy which will help achieve a humane, egalitarian and democratic society. He argues for sociologists' greater involvement in the policy-planning processes.

III

It has been emphasized in recent years that the modern university exists not only to preserve, transmit and extend human knowledge, but to **use** that knowledge to serve humanity. The demands that sociology be relevant to problems of society are being increasingly made by government and non-governmental organizations, and the public. According to Gibbs, (1979) sociologists will avoid collective extinction only by pursuing theories and research that have policy implications. Many sociologists, in recent decades, are increasingly responding to the challenge to be relevant, accepting that the ideal of value-free sociology is hard to achieve. Also, there is a growing conviction that the idea of value- involved but scientifically objective sociology is feasible, important, and useful.

Instead of role segregation between the basic and applied sociologists a role integration — merging the scientist and practitioner role into one — is advocated (Olson and Micklin, 1981: 561-581). Through this role synthesis both basic and applied sociologists become oriented toward answering questions and solving problems that affect the quality of life. Thus, a variety of applied sociological roles include scientific observer-researcher, enlightener, planner, advocate, activist, and policy-maker.

In the "enlightener" role, sociologists not only attempt to provide a new and presumably better understanding of social life but can contribute to policy formation and social change by "challenging the ideas currently in vogue and providing alternative cognitive maps" (Weiss and Bucuvalas, 1977).

The sociologist in the role of planner acts as social engineer. The emphasis is on application rather than research where policy formation is still left to others. Once a policy has been adopted the sociologist as planner undertakes to explore different ways of implementing it.

A sociologist who opts for the role of advocate and activist takes a definite stand on various issues and policies. Without pretending to be value-neutral, sociologists as activists become directly involved in action programs in order to achieve specific goals. The role of sociologists as policy-makers is rarely if ever found, even in the United States, let alone in India and Canada.

Underlying these applied roles of sociologists is the assumption that knowledge carries with it the responsibility to apply it. Nettler (1979: 31-53) raises a fundamental question: "Does the sociologist have a responsibility to make the world a better place?" He thinks that the assumption of such a responsibility is a moral issue that rests on a personal position. His prescription is that sociologists ought to use their knowledge to make the world a better place if they will be responsible for their actions. He observes, however, that sociologists stand on privileged ground that permits criticism and prescription without having to bear the consequences of either. So far, sociologists are seldom, if ever, held responsible for what they teach or advise. Nettler believes that sociologists, by their professional competence and by teaching sociology as one of the humanities can make the world a better place in a few ways.

Nettler leaves open the questions of who is to define the better world and how it is to be achieved. However, he points out that if sociologists become advocates beyond their accountability and professional competence, they will lose what little intellectual authority they have. This question of accountability is rather enigmatic and it is not generally addressed by professional sociological associations. For instance, the professional code of ethics of sociologists published by the A.S.A. (1982) only makes reference to those sociologists working outside of academic settings, it states that they should be aware of possible constraints on research and publication in those settings, and negotiate clear understandings about such conditions accompanying their research and scholarly activity. The issue of accountability of sociologists have not been raised by sociological associations or by governments or other organizations.

These roles of sociologists - teacher, researcher, administrator, consultant, planner, advocate, activist, policy-maker are no doubt open to almost all sociologists although of course many individual sociologists may nevertheless in their lifetime never perform more than one or two of these. For instance, in India and in Canada a large majority of sociologists appear to be primarily teachers and secondarily researchers. Sociologists in the roles of advocates, activists or policy-makers in India and in Canada are indeed hard to find. The professional code of ethics spelled out by the A.S.A. and the C.S.A.A. deal mainly with the role of sociologists as teachers and researchers, and address questions of objectivity and integrity in research, teaching and supervision, student-teacher relations, relationships among sociologists, questions of authorship and acknowledgement, submission of manuscripts for publication, participation in review processes, etc.

IV

During the latter half of the 1960's, however, the American Sociological Association was confronted with demands from young sociologists, committed to their position and oriented toward an academic career, to take particular stands on a number of major issues (Gamson, 1968: Gove, 1970). It was noted (Gove, 1970) that if sociology takes moral stands on political issues, there will be a diminution in both the number and impact of sociologists who do not conform to the dominant political ideology of their profession. Furthermore, even if sociologists hold to a scientific framework, there are issues upon which sociologists qua sociologists can and probably should take stands in the protection of science from regulations that would unjustifiably limit scientific exploration and in indicating some of the consequences of problems and policies.

Many young radical sociologists felt that mainstream sociology's excessive stress on scientific theories - models, methodology, value-free stance are at best irrelevant and at worst a handmaiden of the status quo and a mainstay of the military industrial complex (Kelman, 1970: 77-99). They insisted on the relevance of their research work to significant social issues and recognized that as sociologists their research cannot be value-free.

Moreover, a large amount of sociological research is regarded as a dedicated tool of the status quo. For instance, research on deviant behavior has been more often in terms of the pathology of individuals, than in terms of the characteristics of the larger social system such as the distribution of power, resources and opportunities. Since researchers and research sponsors generally define what is problematic, decide what questions are to be asked and answered within a selected framework, it not only tends to be addressed and applied to the problems perceived by these groups, but is also more likely to support the status quo than to support social change.

Although some sociologists are strongly committed to research that is relevant to social problems and social change, there is a danger in imposing one's definitions of relevance on others.[6] The notion of relevance hinges on one's values and time perspectives; i.e. immediate and long-range or direct or potential applications and implications of sociological knowledge. Therefore, every sociologist, for that matter every social scientist, should have the freedom to pursue his or her own research interests. Also, social research that is supposed to maintain the status quo and that kind of social research with an ideological basis designed to bring about change are no different in using sociology as an instrument to achieve specific goals. In this context, sociologists may indulge in both kinds of research, and it is up to individual sociologists to choose not only a specific topic for research but also the definition, orientation, methodology and relevance to social problems. After all, it is recognized by many that sociology is not necessarily the best training ground for everyone interested in creating social change.

In general, the profession is rather reluctant to allow its patrons to set its research priorities, asserting that sociology should be autonomous, a self-governing polity. However, there is a dilemma concerning the judgment that sociologists should attack immediate social problems with the judgment that they should devote more attention to basic theory. The value judgment that basic research should be conducted without regard to its bearing on social problems has limited validity.

Despite the desire for greater freedom among sociologists, the nature and direction of social research has been influenced by the sources of research support. While discussing some of the ways that research in the social sciences has been affected by the nature and even the sources of research support during the postwar period in the United States, it is stated that increasingly the federal government came to play an important role in funding research and thus in shaping social science priorities'. (R. B. Miller, 1983: 33-35).

Furthermore, Robinson (1983: 35-39) noted the private foundation's role in fostering research in several critical fields, acting as change agents over the 35 years gradually shifting their support from basic to applied research, from building the sciences to using them, and from methodology to multidisciplinary projects.

The research grants and training programs of the National Science Foundation (Riecken, 1983: 39-42) have had a substantial influence on the growth of the social and behavioral sciences in the United States over the last three decades. The policies guiding the selection of research to be supported reflect a view of social science that is epistemologically and methodologically congruent with the position of the physical and biological sciences. In this sense, the influence of NSF has nurtured a science that is positivistic, empirical, quantitative, analytic, value-neutral, and fundamental or basic in orientation.

Brooks (1983: 43-46) observed, 'Sponsorship has more effect on the substantive content and methods of social science research than it does on natural science research. This stems in part from differences actual and perceived, in the relations of the natural and social sciences to public policy and policy makers. In the social sciences, the conceptual structure of knowledge is more intimately connected to the implicit social assumptions and political preferences of the various actors in the policy making process than is the case for the natural sciences.'

It is argued that support for, and the direction of development in the social sciences, are both more directly influenced by current social priorities and attitudes, than is the case with the natural sciences.[7]

In fact, social science research to be eligible for NSF support, according to one 1954 Board Report "should be methodologically rigorous, important for national welfare and defense, convergent with the natural sciences, and characterized by objectivity, verifiability, and generality."

The quest for a 'relevant' Canadian Sociology, for example, raises questions such as: relevant for whom? relevant to what ends? The issue of relevancy of a national sociology is a reaction to the 'value-free' sociology stance that dominated the discipline until recently. In the context of Canadian Sociology, a conception of relevancy, it is suggested (Felt, 1975: 382), is derived from an eclectic, social problems orientation to Canadian society. To be relevant is to work for the improvement of the society. Another conception of relevancy is to engage in social praxis.[8] Some sociologists in India have also raised the issue of relevance and have argued for research that should be relevant to problems of the emancipation of the masses, and have emphasized the need for social praxis. This implies that theoretical understanding must be the basis for action, and such action must dialectically relate to the theoretical understanding.

There seems to be uncertainty as to the possibility and feasibility of a national praxis, given the present state of Canadian Sociology. It is believed that the emergent nationalist feelings open the possibility for creating a number of new sociological paradigms for understanding the society and the potentiality of merging these paradigms with more active participation in the society. The preference is for the development of a number of new and competing Canadian sociologies, each concerned with constructing and elaborating upon a paradigm of the society, thereby stressing the need for multiple paradigms.

The debate on: objectivity-value neutrality vs. value commitment, pure vs. applied sociology, the role of sociologist as observer-analyst vs. planner-change agent revolves around the conception of sociology either as one of the sciences or as one of the humanities.   As opposed to the purely positivist view (represented by, Lazarsfeld, Blalock, Coleman, Schuessler, among others), Bierstedt (1959) claimed that sociology should not be only a science. Rather it must be seen as a bridging discipline between the sciences and humanities; and he contended (1960) that 'not even the scientific sociologist can ultimately escape the ethical and political consequences of his own approach to the problems of society'. He believes that objectivity may not be as desirable a criterion as it is commonly thought to be.

Sociology is in the twilight zone of the humanities and the natural sciences.   As such, researcher's personal values inevitably influence the selection of problems and hypotheses, theories and research methods, the scope of study, interpretation of data and conclusions. These values of researchers are often implicit and concealed which are seldom subject to examination or even known.

The sociology of knowledge maintains that values are defined by particular historical-cultural periods, places and groups. If this view is accepted the crucial problem remains whether some degree of disinterested scientific knowledge is possible. Myrdal (1944, 1969) observed that an implicit belief in the existence of a body of scientific knowledge acquired independently of all valuations is naive empiricism, as facts do not speak or organize themselves except within the framework of concepts and theories that are value-loaded. Thus, the goal to promote sociology in a totally objective manner is an impossible task.   Therefore, neither sociology nor any social science for that matter, can pretend to be 'amoral' or 'apolitical' or neutral or simply factual or totally objective.[9] Under these circumstances Myrdal maintained that by comimg into the open with its basic valuations, social research will become more effective in serving the purpose of intellectual and moral catharsis - which he hoped would contribute to the improvement of society.

Gouldner (1970) made it clear that sociology necessarily operates within the limits of assumptions made by sociologists about society. The use of specific theories and methods imply prior value-assumptions which form part of all social theory and methods.

With reference to a developing society such as India, Varma (1979: 89-102) asserts that social inquiry must be relevant and purposive. The social scientist must have a clear and 'progressive' vision and should take a clearly anti-imperialist stance, and devote his or her energies to the emancipation of the masses from the shackles of colonialism and neo-colonialism.

If sociology is to be relevant for India, Oommen (1983, 1986) argues that it should endorse the value package contained in the Indian Constitution, and through a process of contextualization sociology can play a critical role in the process of national reconstruction as a part of its commitment to human concerns. For him contextualization involves recognition of traditions, present needs and aspirations, adopting appropriate values and institutions from other societies, and judiciously grafting them on to Indian society. He feels that it is necessary to mobilize people to protest against exploitation, injustice and oppression aimed at social transformation. The primary task of Indian sociologists, as perceived by Oommen, is to understand, analyze, and facilitate this process.

Parsons (1959) stated that American sociologists as a profession should prepare themselves for increased pressure stemming from the involvement of sociology in ideological controversy and stressed their responsibility to maintain high standards of scientific competence and objectivity. However, he believed that primary concentration on the science itself is not incompatible with good citizenship in the scientific community and in the general society. The great challenge, according to Parsons, is to maintain the proper balances.

Friederichs (1970) asserts: "Indifference to application (of knowledge) is to be justified by the value-free nature of science is sheer rubbish—but rubbish packaged so attractively and distributed so widely from so many admirable retail outlets that the scientist himself has become a true believer——he is even less aware of its role as a disguise cloaking his self interest than is the general public." According to him pure research is not even in principle value free. It is, rather, an astutely chosen term that reflects the priority granted by the scientist to the satisfaction of one of his own pressing felt needs and the depreciation of non-scientists....Indifference to all but one's own interests is not neutrality. Furthermore, he believes that the search for laws of human nature and for fundamental social processes that are in principle stable is ultimately destined to be futile. The contrast between pure and action research is false. All social research is in principle action research in varying degrees.

Kinloch examined the response of professional sociology to major problems in American society from the 1900s through the 1970s reflected in the annual addresses of presidents of the American Sociological Society/Association. These sociologists have attempted to provide some "objective" basis for solving social problems by effecting greater social harmony through the scientific understanding of social structure. Since the values viewed as effecting such harmony are largely the speaker's own orientations, Kinloch concludes that what may be labelled 'scientific analysis' tends to represent normative projection.

It is suggested (Swedberg, 1980: 232-246) that sociology is not "value free" because this perspective cannot account for the way sociological works are actually generated. By looking at the way communism has been treated in mainstream North American sociology it is noted that the different scholars decided to pursue certain issues rather than others because of their initial opinions of communism. Since most of these studies are strongly anti-communistic, a one sided picture of communism has resulted. Therefore, Swedberg makes a plea for a more sophisticated analysis of the ways in which a scholar is influenced by the society he lives in, so that one might more fully understand the complex relationship between political commitment and social theory.

Gurney (1981: 196-201) shows the relationship between the dominant ideas in early American sociology and the receptivity, opposition, or indifference to the ideas of Karl Marx and concludes that the model response was overwhelmingly negative, and typically along ideological lines, and Marx was defined as beyond the limits of valid inquiry.

It is contended that sociology is most compelling where facts and values cross-fertilize and where informal scholarly investigation provides the point of departure for political and social action. In fact, the camp of radical sociologists claim that sociology faces a power elite bent on converting it into an instrument of domination rather than liberation of humans. It is argued that a truly pluralistic and democratic society requires a basic restructuring of institutions and redistribution of power and wealth; and sociologists cannot just stand aside and hope that it will happen. Instead, they must assume leadership in radical movements and choose the alternative of scientist as partisan of reform rather than as servant and sycophant of the established order.

"During the late 1960s and early 1970s, the social sciences reached a peak of public and political optimism about their capacity to guide peaceful and relatively non controversial "social engineering" on a large scale. Beginning in the late 1960s, and probably partly stimulated by the military interest in and support of the social sciences, a new radical critique of the social sciences became popular, which identified them not with social change and reform but with preserving the status quo and existing power relationships. The notion of value-free social science, and the idea that scholarship could be "neutral" or "impartial", came under severe attack (Gouldner, 1970). It was maintained that the values of the existing distribution of power and status in society are built into the underlying axioms of all the social science disciplines, so that systematic social science research, and particularly quantitative studies, is inherently conservative. Even when the social sciences purport to deal with a variety of options are subtly circumscribed so that choices involving a significant change in the existing power structure are never considered. Thus, government support of the social sciences in the postwar years was at first suspect because it was seen as promoting dangerous social change, but came to be suspect in the minds of many because it was believed to be an instrument for retarding desirable social change. (Brooks, 1983: 43-46).

Friedrichs (1970) maintains, however, that the sociologist qua sociologist has never, even at the height of his doctrinnaire rejection of the valuation process, actually ignored those values in the decisions he made qua sociologist. Furthermore, he posed the question: Can neutrality be an appropriate pose when we are faced with the choice of the issue to be explored? For him the answer must be a completely unambiguous 'no', because pure research is not even in principle value- free as indifference to all but one's own interests is not neutrality.

Sociologists in Canada are considered (Coburn 1970: 37-51) to be relatively inactive and passive as citizens, generally seem closely identified with the 'establishment', have often allowed societal elites to define problems and seldom act as social critics, constructive or otherwise. Above all, it is felt that many English Canadian sociologists lack a strong Canadian identity. Obviously, such a state of affairs has not resulted in active participation of sociologists in societal planning and change processes, despite the increasing recent involvement of some sociologists in policy research.

The roles of values in sociology and their implications for the involvement or lack of involvement of sociologists in social issues, were discussed in the plenary, session on the 'Future of Sociology in Canada', (1970) and the need for greater involvement of sociologists in societally relevant research was stressed. The social science and Humanities Research Council has recently sponsored research in areas such as aging, family and socialization, technology. These themes are supposed to deal with societally relevant contemporary issues in Canadian society.

It is emphasized that the study of Canadian society can and should be approached from a number of perspectives, using different methodologies and data sources. 'But ultimately', as Clement (1977) puts it, 'to have relevance for the study of the national society, they have to be tied into an overriding framework and presumably be aimed at a common concern - such as improving the lot of Canadians, which could mean being concerned about the decline of inequalities of all sorts and the increase and redistribution of the society's resources'.

Watson (1975: 354) questioned the value-neutrality stance of Anglophone Canadian sociologists. He asserted, 'In sociology, at any rate, under some circumstances scholarship purposes may be properly attended to only if the sociologist becomes involved in his subject of inquiry rather than remaining aloof'. It is argued that scientific inquiry is a series of confrontations and refutations which includes values and therefore scientists have a stake in the morality that pervades society. From the standpoint of the sociology of knowledge and the critical theory, the creation and use of sociological knowledge is, in major part, a political process and contains a substantive political content. In contrast to Anglophone sociologists, Francophone sociologists in Canada have been more willing to participate in various non-academic activities, and as effective social critics they are more involved in dealing with problems of Quebec society. This distinct activist and radical style of French Canadian sociology seems to stem from its social action origins and strong nationalistic aspirations. Rocher (1977) asserts that the sociologist is increasingly an agent of historical change, and, in the future, he is destined to play an even more active and important role; and he hopes that Francophone sociologists will exert more influence, not only inside but also outside Quebec.

V

Lynd (1939) identified the emphasis on objectivity, empirical positivism and value-free analysis. He urged sociologists for more involved and pragmatic research. This debate on objective vs. committed research has been a perennial topic of controversy in the social sciences. Positivists and neo-positivists in sociology support objective knowledge and value-free stance whereas critical and radical sociologists and humanists (Mills, Myrdal, Gouldner) believe that sociology should be for the service of humanity.

Furthermore, it is argued (Lee, 1978) that the character of any sociological inquiry depends upon by whom and for whom it is carried out. The dominant sociologists tend to obtain a hold upon more of the discipline and shore up the legitimacy of their kind of sociology. American sociologists, caught up in the practical exigencies of careerism, are not only almost always limited in their research by professionalism but also act like 'robots' to meet the mandates of the market place. According to Lee, the excuse for the existence of sociologists is not simply the maintenance of academic employment and research funding. Sociology for the service of humanity should develop knowledge of direct service to all classes of people and it should be communicated through all appropriate media. Sociology includes studies of ways in which people can protect themselves from undesirable manipulation by those in positions of power, and of how to enhance the quality of life. It is in this context that sociologists in serving humanity act principally as critics, demystifiers, reporters, and clarifiers, enabling people to understand human relations and to cope with personal and social problems.

On the one hand, it is stressed (Wilson 1971: 576-586) that knowledge is a form of power, and in a society increasingly dependent on knowledge, the control of information creates the potential for political manipulation. Sociologists tend to produce an ever less approximate knowledge of social reality that seems to become a new form of 'capital'. It has the potential to be used by the political and economic elite to serve their vested interests. For these reasons, the sociologist must be responsible, first and foremost, to the truth of his investigation. Sociology must not be an instrument of any person or group who seeks to suppress or misuse knowledge. The fate of sociology, as a science is considered dependent upon the fate of free inquiry in an open society.

Be that as it may, radical-humanists forcefully state that sociologists have a special competence which entitles them - indeed, from a moral perspective compels them - to take authoritative positions on social issues such as: poverty, exploitation, racism, sexism, and war. Almost every sociologist faces the challenge of social action and the challenge of social policy. But Nisbet (1970:402) observed that there is another more compelling truth that 'any science will be helpful, pertinent, and relevant in the long run only to the extent that it is left alone to pursue its unique and vital objectives of discovery and explanation'.

Given these opposing viewpoints of the role of values in sociology, undoubtedly, there is a need to strike a balance between the demands of ivory tower attitude of aloofness; i.e. a value free stance and value-involvement or direct action. Sociologists' personal experience and values will influence which way they lean in their professional and non-professional roles. In any event, it seems that value judgments cannot be avoided and total objectivity cannot be maintained by sociologists.

Hamnett (1984) and his colleagues examine the process and ethics of cross-national social science research, especially as it

involves scholars from Western industrialized countries and their
collaborators and subjects from the Third World. They focus on
two key issues: the degree to which researchers from
industrialized countries have an obligation to collaborate with
scholars from the less industrialized countries they study and the
degree to which researchers are obliged to ensure that their
subjects benefit from research.

Although the authors believe that scientific research holds
the promise of resolving social problems and bettering human life,
they are critical of traditional approaches to research.   In
particular they are concerned about the shortcomings of
value-neutral inquiry.   As an alternative, they propose
collaboration: a style of interaction they have used successfully
in their own research.   They insist, however, that alternative
approaches should be integrative and consistent through all levels
of concern — ideological, theoretical, and practical.   Their aim
is to unify theory and practice in — and create a praxis of —
social science research ethics. How the future sociologists will
meet this challenge and resolve the value-objectivity dilemma
remain to be seen in the next decade and the next century.

CHAPTER 7

INTERNATIONAL AND NATIONAL SOCIOLOGIES
PROBLEMS AND PROSPECTS

What role can national sociologies play in the development of universal sociology? What factors account for the effects of nationality on the sociological task and prevent us from seeing sociology as universally the same? What are the channels of communication between national and international sociologies that can lead to the enrichment of the discipline of sociology both within and across nations? Can sociology be nation-free? What is the future of sociology? These questions deserve our attention.

I

Thus far we have noted the predominant influence of American sociology on the sociologies of India and Canada. It is also evident that Indian sociology is more distinguishable than Canadian sociology when compared to American sociology. This is because of cultural similarities and differences and geographic proximity and distance of Canada and India from the U.S. Furthermore, we have also observed the emergence of a movement aimed at the indigenization of sociology in India and Canada. This indigenization movement tends to be a response to American imperialism (academic, political, economic, etc.), the desire to be relevant to national issues and contexts and nationalistic sentiments. However, American sociology and sociologists still serve as the reference group for a majority of sociologists in India, Canada and elsewhere.

Where do we go from here? Or rather, where should we go? Sociology, ideally at least, has been claimed, by the founding fathers as well as by contemporary sociologists, to be a universal science. However in actuality, sociology, by and large, has been nationalistic in content and orientation. Wolff (1946) suggested that American sociology is not so much a science or a discipline as it is an orientation that reflects a culture and that demands a socio-cultural orientation. Moore (1966: 477), Shils (1970: 702), Friedrichs (1970), and Gouldner (1970) have demonstrated that American sociology developed, both quantitatively and qualitatively, identifying with American values and culture. Likewise, the cultural milieu in India (Clinard and Elder, 1965; Nandy, 1971; Chekki, 1978) has shaped Indian sociology. The development of Canadian sociology (Vallee and Whyte, 1968; Connor and Curtis, 1970; Forcese and Richer, 1975, 1982; Hiller, 1979) has been subject to historical and cultural forces emanating from within Canada.

What we have tried to show is that not only the internal forces characteristic of a nation but also external forces - i.e. the influence of American sociology[1] (it's hegemony as world's leading economic- military power) have played an important role in the development of Sociology in India and Canada, especially after World War II, thus creating dependency of the latter on the former. The emulation of American sociological theories and methods by sociologists in India and Canada was facilitated through an increasing use of American sociology text books, research monographs, and journals as well as through training programs and research scholarship provided by American government and private foundations.

Despite these American influences characteristic of the 1950s and 1960s, both India and Canada began to react to this process of Americanization of their sociologies. The process of de-Americanization started a little earlier in India than in Canada. However, both India and Canada seem to have followed a similar course in their process of indigenization of national sociologies, in that they have reacted to the inappropriateness or lack of relevance of concepts, theoretical approaches, and methodologies characteristic of American sociology.

There is a growing desire on the part of both Indian and Canadian sociologists to develop their own theoretical models, traditions and perspectives - from the point of view of the insider - for studying their societies and problems. Nationalism, latent forms of ethnocentrism, and the imperialistic tendencies of American sociology, it appears, have given impetus to the development of a nationally relevant sociology in India and Canada. Similar trends are apparent in other countries as well (Baldock and Lally, 197 4; Gardezi, 1975).

This quest for national sociologies with their own theoretical approach and a capacity to deal with problems unique to a nation is not considered to be in contradiction to the ideal of universal science of sociology. It is pointed out (Hiller, 1979: 128) that national sociologies are not so much an attack on American sociology as they are at heart an attack on sociology as a universal value-free discipline. These national sociologies seem to point out the relativism of the science.

Hiller (1979: 128-131) identified three factors that help to account for the effects of nationality on the sociological task and that prevent us from seeing sociology as universally the same.

1) Differences in dominant ideologies: National ideological concerns such as capitalism, individualism, rationalism,

liberalism, competitiveness, egalitarianism, achievement ethic, fear of communism in developing countries have no doubt influenced the nature of sociology in America. In India the dominant religious-philosophical **Weltanschauung** of Dharma, Karma, Moksha, etc. have in major part influenced Indian sociology. Sociology in Canada, however, has developed not so much as the result of its value differences, but because of nationalism, the fear of Canadians being absorbed in to the U.S., and the subsequent attempts at differentiation (Anderson et al, 1975: Hiller, 1979). More importantly, in all these three countries sociology has been influenced by government and other institutional supports through the funding of higher institutes of learning and research where sociology thrives and flourishes.

2) Differences in the institutionalization of the discipline: We have already shown why sociology was institutionalized successfully earlier and relatively rapidly as a teaching and research discipline in American universities, but later and more slowly in Indian and Canadian universities. Even today the quantitative growth of sociology in India and Canada cannot match that of American sociology. The reasons are quite obvious, as discussed earlier and require no further elaboration at this stage.

The way sociology has developed in universities, the way it is linked to other disciplines, to governments, non-governmental organizations, and the public varies substantially among these three nations. The importance assigned to social problems, national needs, government policies, conceptions and values associated with social science have influenced the manner in which sociology was institutionalized and in turn shaped sociology in America, India and Canada.

3) Differences in national development: Madge (1968), Aron (1971: 165) and others have observed that industrialization has been the basic theme of sociology and that the differences in sociologies between countries are related to different forms and patterns of modernization and change. Sociologies of America, India, and Canada are good illustrations of how the different forms, patterns, and time sequence of industrialization, urbanization, economic and political development and change processes have moulded national sociologies. It is assumed that this inter-linkage between modernization and sociology will not only bring some similarities in social analysis but also certain characteristics of American sociology would be essential to every sociology as modernization progresses in other countries. In this sense, (Aron, 1971) all sociologies will become Americanized. But do they? Our analysis suggests that they do not, at least in the long run.

Despite the degree of homogenization of sociology, differences in national sociologies cannot be underestimated. Coburn (1970: 39) cautions that 'we should be aware of equating what is American with what is universal. Sociologists in India and Canada, while analyzing the process of modernization in their own countries, have reacted to a state of academic dependency and tended to indigenize sociology in a national rather than a comparative way (Hiller, 1979: 131), primarily because of national differences in dominant ideologies, institutional features and development processes. On the one hand, national sociologies are considered to be culture-bound, ethnocentric, and parochial. In this respect a national sociology insulated from sociologies in other countries is myopic and impoverished (Merton, 1959) and it is far from being a universal science. On the other hand, national sociologies are recognized as both necessary and inevitable for their significant role in providing a more complete analysis of social life within specific national contexts, as long as sociology takes place in national contexts.

Somewhat paradoxically, as Hiller (1979) put its, national sociologies have the potential to reducing ethnocentrism at the same time they seem to create it. In stressing the need for a society-specific sociology, Mukherjee (1971: 367) states that universality of science has not been attained in any discipline without an objective comprehension of its particular manifestations. After all, national sociologies are expected to eventually reduce ethnocentrism by enriching and strengthening our concepts and theories. This is possible when national sociologies frequently continue to maintain contact with sociologies in other countries, and sociologists indulge in comparative analysis of research data, as well as examining theoretical perspectives emanating from different countries.

Sociology claims to be a universal science to the extent that it possesses globally similar rules of scientific logic and procedure. The goal of theory building based on cross-cultural comparative research also establishes the claim of sociology as a universal discipline. However, one cannot ignore or underestimate the importance of the diversity and complexity of societies and cultures which are hard to explain with universalistic or grand theories. Therefore, sociology i.e. global, universal or international sociology tends to gain more by the prevalence of national sociologies that focus on the meaning and dynamics of social phenomena in a specific national context. Universalistic theory can be formulated, tested and revised on the basis of cross-national comparative data, analysis and codification. It is in this context that national sociologies and international sociology can be mutually contributing, enriching the discipline of sociology both within and across nations. In this sense, the question of whether sociology can be nation-free becomes redundant. The sociology of sociologies and the sociology of

knowledge can periodically undertake a critical review of the
status of concepts, theories and methods in sociology in different
countries and may help reduce provincialism or nationalism by
facilitating the process of the internationalization of scholarly
dialogue in sociology.

Bottomore and Nisbet (1978: xiv) identify two trends in the
recent development of sociological analysis that merit preliminary
attention at this stage. First there is the growth and
consolidation, during the past two or three decades, of an
international scientific community within which, in spite of the
diversity of viewpoints upon which we have insisted, the active
exchange and criticism of ideas and research findings have the
effect of defining more clearly the boundaries of the discipline
and the set of problems that constitutes its subject matter. To
this extent at least it may be claimed that there is now a single
discipline, a realm of scientific discourse outside of which
sociological analysis cannot properly be pursued at all; and this
discipline — at once the product and the binding element of a
community of scientists which sets itself distinct and specified
aims ——— constitutes a relatively autonomous sphere which is
perhaps increasingly resistent to purely ideological influences.

A second trend is closely associated with this development;
namely, the movement away from 'national' schools of sociology,
and from the creation of highly individual sociological systems,
which were characteristic of an earlier period. Of course, some
elements of the previous conditions remain. Even though there are
no longer any very distinctive 'national' schools of sociology,
there is still a 'regional' preeminence of European and North
American sociology in the **discipline as a whole**. But who can
forsee with any confidence what further transformation of
sociological analysis will occur as it develops in the context of
different cultural traditions and other civilizations? (Bottomore
and Nisbet, 1978: xiv).

The International Sociological Association has recently
(1986) commenced publication of a new quarterly journal entitled
"International Sociology". Its purpose is to present
international sociological analysis made by sociologists from
diverse cultural traditions and national origins. This new forum,
facilitating cross-cultural fertilisation of sociological research
and networks linking sociologists from various countries and
theoretical traditions, could pave the way toward developing a
truly international sociology. Tiryakian (1986:155-171) asserts
that "Macro-sociology must drop the parochialism of implicitly
confining itself to intra-state phenomena, based on western
historical experience, and develop a conceptual framework adequate
to deal with the emergent transnational global structures and
processes of change. To achieve this goal, he recommends, an
internationalisation of the sociology curriculum at both

undergraduate and graduate levels. He believes this would contribute to sociology's great leap forward in establishing an international sociology in the next century.

II
What about the future of sociology? There are many speculations, predictions, and aspirations expressed by sociologists. Some of these futuristic comments are based on recent and contemporary trends and projections of these trends while other indications are primarily sociologists' reflections of personal values as to what national or international sociology should be in the future.

We have noted that sociology in India, besides developing its own characteristics, has also responded to various theoretical and methodological approaches emanating from the U.S. The discipline is said to be at the threshold of a new process of theoretical and methodological integration, but its structure and direction are not yet well crystallized. A particularistic brand of Indian sociology, as advocated by some Indian sociologists, remains merely a form of empty dialectics, as no systematic codification of its eventual form has so far been spelled out (Singh, 1967). It is believed that the prospect for sociology in India lies in a continued tradition of research based on a variety of methods and intellectual orientations.

With the emergence of new issues and problems and new demands on the discipline, it is expected that sociology in India will be shaped by new and continuing forces arising in India and abroad. Clinard and Elder (1965: 587) speculated that during the coming decades a major factor in the development of a body of cross-cultural sociological generalizations will be the maintenance of a continual dialogue between the sociologists of India and those of other countries.

"Out of the diverse perspectives and methods which characterize sociology in India today," remarked Nandy (1971: 142), the consensus which can optimistically be expected in the sociology of India tomorrow will depend fundamentally on increasing agreement on its subject matter, theoretical formulations, and methods of inquiry. Indian sociology, without becoming a replica of the sociology of any other country, has a tendency to exhibit a synthesis of modes of inquiry and of perspectives, and it is hoped that it will contribute its share to the development of a world sociology.

During the 1980s the present trends in Indian sociology seem to continue. Government sponsored and financed research will emphasize problems of national importance. Issues pertaining to socio-econonic development, and in particular a stress on disadvantaged groups will receive priority for research. However, cross-cultural comparative research and theoretical inquiries will not be totally neglected either. Namboodari (1980) thinks that it would be a major contribution to international sociology if one could bridge East and West at a level of abstraction high enough to embrace both Hindu and Christian culture. M.S.A. Rao (1982) thinks that in the 1980s sociology will develop into a policy science only if the sociologists accept the challenge of making more significant breakthroughs in policy research. According to Y.B. Damle (1982) the sociologist's task in the 1980s would be to analyze the transformation of Indian society.

T.K.N. Unnithan (1982) maintains that 'Old Sociology' was the product of colonialism and conservation and should be discarded. The 'New Sociology' in India, he argues, should have at its centre the power of love and compassion; it should be what he calls a 'transcendental sociology' that tries to break conceptual barriers and segmental interests and concentrates on the collective question of promoting love, compassion and altruism, i.e a sociology that will be of help to the poor and the suffering. P. K. B. Nayar (1982) identifies five tasks for the sociologist: develop sociology as a policy science, be actively involved in social problems, play the role of social critic, foster multi- disciplinary approach, and develop social indicators to measure program achievements.

The long term underdevelopment of sociology in Canada was no doubt followed by recent efforts to nationalize and develop Canadian sociology. Despite a growing movement advocating a distinct Canadian sociology, there is still much that remains to be done toward developing a sociology that can be distinguished as Canadian. It is speculated (Anderson et al. 1975) that the future of Canadian sociology may take one of many directions. It may (i) continue to be a mutilated form of American sociology; (ii) develop as an indigenous product focusing on Canadian society with its unique problems; (iii) end up as an amalgam of the other two tendencies; (iv) become independent of the pressures of external domination and realize its evolutionary potential. This possibility of Canadian sociology having its own theoretical frameworks and perspectives is considered to be remote.

Forcese and Richer (1975: 447) think that Canadian sociology will develop a style of its own avoiding the unthinking importation of assumptions and explanations from another country. They aspire to have a Canadian sociology inspired by and sensitive to pertinent i.e. 'real and important' Canadian social problems. For them (Forcese and Richer, 1982: 7) the repudiation of American sociology has been expressed in the revival of the Marxian-influenced neo-political economy perspective. in Canadian sociology. It is anticipated that eventually distinctive orientations will emerge in Canadian sociology. Though it is impossible to predict whether there will be an emergence of a

Canadian sociological style that integrates the Francophone and Anglophone traditions, it is hoped that Canadian sociology will consist at least in part of an action issues orientation characteristic of French Canadian sociology.

The future of Canadian sociology, according to Clement (1977), will depend upon its keeping up with current trends and being able to place them within the context of the national society. More importantly, it is expected that tomorrow's sociologist will have to be constantly critical of the values which inspire and motivate and influence his/her research and interventions. It is believed (Rocher, 1977) that the future will require of the sociologist a more acute perception of the exigencies of his/her intervention in society and of the epistomological and ethical consequences of such intervention.

While expecting an increased development of a more distinctly Marxist and radical sociology, Gouldner (1970: 443-66) suggested a future trend in American sociology will be a continuing drift of functionalism toward Marxism, but without the possibility of blending or convergence. As far as the structure of academic sociology with respect to its theoretical ideological ramifications are concerned, he felt that it will become much more polycentric than it has been so far.

American sociology, as we noted earlier, has remained a multistrategy field having a marked effect on the cumulative growth of sociological knowledge. There are seemingly irreconcilable conflicts pertaining to meta-theoretical questions involving matters of value as well as matters of fact. According to Zelditch (1979), the likely prospect is that American sociology will remain a stable multistrategy field for the forseeable future - meaning at least till 2000 A.D.

Schuessler (1979: 31-35) forecasts that in the year 2000 American sociology will be more empirical, less apriori; more specific, less general; more practical, less academic. The relation of social problems to sociology will be more open and above board. Sociology will be more slanted toward public policy and social legislation. There will be more money for research and development in sociology. The importance of sociology will be judged more by its cost effectiveness than by its theoretical insights and understandings. Statistical methodology will be even more dominant and the effects of the computer will be everywhere by the year 2000. Measurement and time series will have a higher priority as sociology moves toward the next century. Because of diverging concerns, schools of sociology will be more sharply separated, in both program and membership.

By the year 2000 the supply of sociology Ph.D.'S will be larger in absolute terms, smaller relative to all persons doing sociology, and they will count relatively more women and non-whites in their ranks. Sociology will continue to attract persons of strong social consciousness. In graduate school students will be trained more, educated less, spending more time on the computer and less time reading in the library. Sociologists will be more at home among scientists and will stand higher with the general public. Such forecasts based on present trends and the forecaster's values and aspirations tend to indicate some of the possible directions that American sociology might take in the next two decades leading to the twenty-first century. These projected changes in American sociology will have some repercussions on sociologies in India and in Canada. The nature of the impact of American sociology on other national sociologies and thereby on international sociology will of course depend upon how national sociologies (other than American) will respond to American sociology. We have to wait until the 21st century for an evaluation of trends in the growth of national sociologies during the years ahead. Until then sociologists are no doubt destined to play an active and important role. As Parsons (1968) put it, 'our science may well be destined to play a major role, not only in its primary task of understanding the social and cultural world we live in as object of its investigations, but, in ways which cannot be foreseen, in actually shaping the world.'

A review of the problems and prospects of American sociology (Short, 1981) notes progress in terms of convergence of approaches, advances in quantitative methods, and expanded data bases. It is believed that future progress in developing cumulative knowledge will be highly dependent on the combination of formal theory and methods, because presently most cumulative work remains largely empirical rather than theoretical. In view of the fact that specialties within the discipline often ignore developments within the mainstream, and because of sectarian and ideological tendencies, a plea for collegiality is made.

CHAPTER 8

WHITHER SOCIOLOGY?

This juxtaposition of national sociologies of the United States, India, and Canada has highlighted some of the similarities, differences, unique features, interactions, influences and dominant trends in sociology. The foregoing analysis suggests that there are different kinds of sociologies within and across nations. American sociology has been influential on sociologies of most of the non-communist countries, as exemplified in the sociologies of India and Canada. The flow of influence is in one direction, that is, from the United States to other countries and not vice versa. Furthermore, sociologies of India and Canada manifest trends of dependency on American sociology.

The relevance of American Sociology is being increasingly questioned in India and Canada and the process of indigenization of the national sociologies of the latter seems to be partly a response to the domination of the former and partly a result of differences in national cultural milieux. It appears that national sociologies, despite some efforts, have not as yet been successful in overcoming the dominance of American sociological theory and methods in that there are as yet no significant developments of theories and methods appropriate to each national milieu.

Whether such nation-specific concepts, theories, and methodology are necessary is altogether a different question which cannot be discussed here at this stage, though relevant and important. A large majority of sociologists in both India and Canada still consider consciously or unconsciously, American sociology and sociologists as their 'significant others' or reference group. Given the fact of American domination in world sociology, questions are raised as to the role and need for national sociologies in the development of a universal science of sociology.

In the United States, India and Canada macro-level Weberian-Parsonian and Marxist theoretical orientations are in the fore-front of confrontation and controversy whereas micro-level theories such as symbolic interactionism, exchange theory, and ethnomethodology are not of great concern, at least in India and Canada.

Based on the evidence presented so far, we do not wish to offer the simplistic proposition that prevalent ideological considerations determine the nature and content of sociological knowledge and practice. On the contrary, our analysis of the development of sociologies in the U.S., India, and Canada demonstrates a process of reciprocity and dialectics between ideological and social forces both within and across nations.

Parsons' and Bierstedts' thesis that ideas are relatively autonomous in the stream of history and are more dependent upon antecedent ideas than they are upon the social, economic, or political circumstances of the times finds limited support, if any, from our study. It is evident that sociology as an academic discipline and profession has evolved and developed not only as a result of its own inner dialectics-dynamics of ideas but also in response to socio- economic-political conditions and forces that have been in existence over time, both within and outside a nation.

Furthermore, whether we like it or not, there are different traditions, schools, and varieties of shades of sociologies within and across nations. Given the belief and aim of a universal science of sociology, it is most likely that in the future such a diversity in sociology will continue. As Merton (1959) aptly put it: "The extent of heterodoxies among the sociologists of each nation has an important bearing on the future development of world sociology. The heterodoxies in one nation provide intellectual linkages with orthodoxies in other nations. On the worldwide scale of sociology, this bridges lines of cleavage and makes for the advance of sociological science rather than of sociological ideologies."

We have noted some of the dominant streams of sociology in America and how sociologies of India and Canada have been influenced by American sociology. Simultaneously, it is shown that each country manifests different degrees of heterodoxy in sociological thought and styles of sociological work, and these differences are socially patterned.

Most sociologists are undoubtedly engaged in intellectual controversy and conflict pertaining to theoretical, methodological, and substantive issues. In addition, sociologists are also involved in social conflict and status battles regarding the allocation of intellectual resources among different kinds of sociological work, often accusing one another of engaging in the study of 'trivia' instead of 'significant problems'. It is projected that the variations in sociological orientations - in terms of theories, methodologies, substantive areas, and meta-theoretical issues - will continue along with distinct national sociologies which, we hope can make unique contributions to international sociology.

The sociology of knowledge thesis developed by Marx, Mannheim, Merton and Coser, among others, that the development of sociological knowledge is related to the socio-economic and political conditions of the society in which it emerges is further reinforced by this comparative analysis of national sociologies. More importantly, from the foregoing evidence it is quite obvious that the dependency and world system model finds adequate support from this study in the American sociology constituting the "core" has had considerable power and influence in creating a state of dependency on the part of the "peripheral" and "semi-peripheral" sociologies of India and Canada.

It is important to recognize, however, that no single explanatory model is entirely comprehensive even though all these models in conjunction seem to be useful for an adequate understanding of the growth of sociology in different national contexts.

The institutional, ideological, and contextual models used in our analysis of the development of sociology in the United States, India, and Canada do emphasize the importance of these variables and the intricate interrelationships of these forces in influencing the patterns of growth or lack of growth of sociology, especially in India and Canada.

Supported by the economic and political power of the state, numerous sociologists in the United States have been engaged in teaching, research, publication, and practice. Consequently, in the vertical mosaic of international sociology, American sociology that has been exerting a great influence on the national sociologies of those societies that have lesser resources and opportunities than those of the United States.

The decades of the 1950s and 1960s were the heydays of American sociology's dominant influence abroad. Howver, in the 1970s this American hegemony seemed to be steadily waning because of the process of nationalization of sociology in India and Canada, and also because of considerable reduction of various foreign-aid programs (particularly in the fields of education, research, and exchange of scholars) by the United States.

Moreover, in recent years the sociologies of India and Canada have been making concerted efforts to develop their own theoretical orientations appropriate to their social milieu. How far they will succeed in this endeavor still remains to be seen. In any event, such efforts by sociologists in different nations will, it is hoped, eventually reduce the hegemonic influence of American sociology. It is in this context that we make a strong plea for cross-national comparative research and the development of a universal sociology that is enriched by national sociologies.

It is necessary to have a continuing communication and dialogue, instead of insularity and isolation, among national sociologies. This mutual interaction, codification of cross-national empirical data, and macro-level theorizing would facilitate the development of universal sociology. Current and continuing efforts in this direction, let us hope, will lead to a well developed universal sociology in the twenty first century.

1. A review (Lengerman, 1974) of the views of Comte,
Spencer, Marx, Durkheim, Weber, Simmel, Mead, Pareto on the
subject matter of sociology states that sociology, according to
these earlier sociologists, attempts the scientific study of
social life.

There seems to be no such consensus among contemporary
sociologists. Although Nisbet (1970) considers sociology as a
science primarily concerned with discovery and explanation he
thinks that the ultimate goal of every science is that of being
relevant to the social and material needs of human beings. He
concludes, however, that any science will be helpful, pertinent,
and relevant in the long run only to the extent that it is left
alone to pursue its unique and vital objectives of discovery and
explanation.

McDaniel and Agger (1983) representing another extreme view
define sociology as a problem-seeking and problem-solving social
science. To this extent, it is impossible to practice sociology
at all without being concerned with social problems and social
change. In this sense it is not value free.

2. 'The history of sociological analysis is useful in
various ways. First, a historical study that takes into account
the social and cultural context in which a particular body of
theoretical ideas has developed should enable us to discriminate
more precisely between the evolution of the theoretical concepts
and propositions themselves, and the influence upon them of
various social and cultural interests or in other words, to
distinguish between the scientific and the ideological content of
a system of sociological thought.

Second, because the objects of sociological analysis include
not only universal characteristics of human societies but also
historical and changing phenomena, a history of the various
approaches and theories reveals the extent to which many of them,
at least in some respects, have a restricted and specific scope in
as much as they deal with the facts and problems of particular
historical periods. In this respect, however, there may be quite
substantial differences between theories in different areas of
sociology.' (Bottomore and Nisbet, 1978: xiv)

3. Coser and Lengermann, among several others, have shown
how ideas of sociologists were shaped by the social and political
events of their day and how nationality and language influence the
pattern of communication among sociologists.

4. Sherman and Wood (1979) emphasize the need for a unified social science and view social arrangements from the perspective of oppressed groups and consider possible alternatives to the present social organization. Throughout the book traditional structural-functional approach is contrasted with radical neo-Marxian-political economy approach.

5. Sociological ideas are seen to articulate certain crucial dilemmas of the day, both influencing social context and in turn being influenced by it. Sociologies both reflect current attitudes towards issues in a society and at the same time affect those attitudes. (McDaniel and Agger, 1983: 3).

6. According to Lazarsfeld (1969) American sociologists should know more about sociology abroad not only for the purpose of a comparison of findings and problems but also it makes them realize the influence of American Sociology abroad.

2
TOWARDS A SOCIOLOGY OF SOCIOLOGIES

1. (Bottomore and Nisbet, 1978), sociology, however vast, unwieldy, and liable to extremely varied conceptualizations, has developed alternative paradigms and theoretical controversy through the accumulation of an ordered body of knowledge resulting from empirical research directed by one or another paradigm and through the specialization of research.

2. Among sociologists of knowledge there is a widespread agreement that some kind of extistential relationship exists between knowledge and social bases.

3. According to Karl Mannheim the social sciences are inescapably ideological. What they produce is not scientific theories which can be tested and rationally evaluated, even though they contain such elements as empirical data and rational systematization, but doctrines, which formulate the interests and aspirations of various social groups, among them nations, ethnic groups, and cultural groups, as well as social classes. From this point of view, the movements of thought in Sociology depend upon developments in society and culture, and the waxing and waning of sociological theories have to be accounted for by the varying fortunes of different social groups in their ceaseless competition and conflict.

The idea that sociological analysis is essentially ideological has been presented in quite diverse ways, ranging from a sociology of knowledge to a Hegelian-Marxist philosophy of history. "Sociology has aspired to the status of the widest ranging, the most general of the social sciences, but ended up as the most fragmented of them all." (the discipline wanted to pose

as the queen, it ended up as the clown of the sciences of man.)
(Crawford and Rokkan, 1976: 9)

3
PARADIGMS AND HEGEMONY

1. G.H. Page in a Foreword to Hinkle's (1954) 'The Development of Modern Sociology' states, 'From the beginning, sociology in the U.S. has been largely a product of native conditions. The role of changing American culture and social structure in the development of modern sociology is itself an important sociological lesson. The changing emphasis in the conception of the nature of the subject and of its appropriate tasks, in concrete investigatory problems, and even in method reflect, directly and indirectly, such major features of the American historical experience as the frontier and its closure, urbanization and industrialization, large-scale immigration, political democracy and antidemocratic developments, ever extending public education, deeply rooted Christian doctrine, growing bureacratization in more and more areas, and, not least, two world wars and the Great Depression.

Hinkle and Hinkle (1954) provide a panoramic view of the major changes & identifying landmarks of American sociology over the last 50 years. They observed that although American sociology is a product of both European and native intellectual influences, the discipline is uniquely American in organization and development. It is pointed out that the outstandingly persistent feature of American sociology is its voluntaristic nominalism. They attempt to show that the intellectual content of sociology is related to and dependent on its social context - the organization of professional sociologists, broader intellectual current, and the larger social and cultural setting. While it does not pretend to be a sociology of sociology, it does try to make the student aware that the nature of sociology is not merely the result of a self-contained development, unaffected by trends outside the discipline itself.

During its first half century American sociology increasingly diversified its problems of investigation, specialized its methods and refined its generalizations and theories. These developments were in part reflection of the process of urbanization and centralization of American society and a response to the critical events of two world wars and a nationwide economic depression.

2. Hollander (1981: 22) estimates that probably close to 90 percent of the research done (and courses taught) deal with substantive issues in the American context alone; 10-15 percent of the work may involve non-American case studies sometimes equated with comparative sociology; the remaining five percent or so may be divided between comparisons of several non-American cases and

those which contrast some American with the non-American. It is suggested that comparative sociology, and primarily its cross-cultural or cross-national variety, has remained on the margins of American sociology.

3. Friedrichs presents two major paradigms in American Sociology: The First order dominant paradigm trends 1) Prophetic dominance prior to world war II, 2) Priestly dominance from about 1947 to 1962; and 3) Prophetic dominance from around 1963 to 1970. The second order trends are - 1) Pre-paradigmatic condition until world war II; 2) The system paradigm until the early sixties; 3) The conflict paradigm from the midsixties onwards.

Gouldner delineates 4 major periods in the development of Western sociology: 1) Sociological positivism, 2) Marxism, 3) Classical sociology, 4) Parsonian structual-functionalism leading to Marxist & neo Marxist conflict sociology in the sixties. Finally, sociology becoming polycentrist with diverse theoretical perspectives. Bottomore and Nisbet (1978) observed, 'The multiplicity of paradigms in sociology reflect manifestly wide-ranging controversies about the nature and validity of sociology as such. We cannot claim that there is some universally accepted conception of the object of sociological analysis which provides the context for every theoretical dispute. This uncertainty, the lurking presence of radically opposed, or in commensurable, images of man and society in the background of diverse theoretical schemes, presents major difficulties with regard to resolving disagreements, moving from one paradigm to another, or evaluating scientific progress in sociology.'

'Wilbert E. Moore (1981) states, 'My sense of the course of American sociology for the last several decades is not that of ideological polarization but rather of ideological and substantive fragmentation.'

I believe that the disarray I perceive within American sociology owes much to a loss of unifying themes, interest, and shared theoretical orientations.

Edward Shils observed that sociology "as a heterogeneous aggregate of topics is held together by a more or less common tradition - a heterogeneous one to which certain currents stand out-linked to common monuments or classical figures or works."

4. According to Lantz (1984) the proliferation of new sociological areas and journals may suggest that sociology is becoming everything and anything. He raised the question, 'Are we in danger of becoming a sociology of special interest groups, each pleading its own cause?'

5. Lantz (1984) 'While the ideological character of sociology is ever present, ideology affords us the opportunity to note the incomplete nature of our understanding of society. It allows us to develop the method and data that lead to new paradigms that may result in generalizations about societies and social structures. While this may take place, ideology can also have negative effects on authors and the field at any time.'

6. Gouldner states, 'When viewed from one stand point 'methodology seems a purely technical concern devoid of ideology; presumably it deals only with methods of extracting reliable information from the world, collecting data, constructing questionnaires, sampling, and analyzing returns.' However, he argues that, 'Every research method makes some assumptions about how information may be secured from people and what may be done with people, or to them, in order to secure it; this, in turn, rests on certain domain assumptions concerning who and what people are.'

7. Lantz (1984) addressing the issue of the character of sociology and its relationship to the changes in American sociology observes a major shift in the sociological perspective during the early 1960s, when sociologists began to focus systematically on how society came to define, label, isolate, and oppress those without power who manifested perceived problems.

8. Writing about studies in social stratification in Australia and New Zealand, Baldock and Lally (1975: 461-63) state: "Researchers who neglect theoretical models often tend to replicate American research, and in the process, usually adopt - perhaps unwittingly - a functionalist framework". This influence is also felt in the folds of political sociology and sociology of education in Australia as well.

9. In a survey of sociological research in Britain Krausz, (1969) notes that most of the studies are problem-oriented; methods and techniques used in empirical research seems to be American.

For purposes of comparative analysis it would be useful to note that changes in British society contributed to developments of particular areas of sociology. For instance Abrams et al (1981) focused on developments in and reflections about British Sociology. During the period 1950-1980 they noticed several changes not only in the theories, methodologies and research practices of the discipline, but also in the institutional setting of sociology. These changes have reflected shifting perspectives and concerns within the discipline and they have also been closely linked to the history of British society as a whole which has affected the kinds of sociological problems that are felt to require investigation as well as emphasizing the power of certain modes of explanation and analysis at the expense of others.

There have, specially since the 1960s, been links between developments in sociology and many forms of popular politics, such as the early 'New Left', the women's and students' movements, black power and several counter-cultural movements.

The effects of these popular movements on the growth of particular areas of sociology of education, political sociology, women's studies have been considerable, but there have also been more far reaching consequences for sociology as a whole, pushing it more and more in the direction of at least examining the relation between knoweldge and action and, for example, of attempting to remove the patriarchal and sexist shaping of such sociological work.

The feminist intervention in sociology has been particularly important becaust it has been able to how how one-sided the theories and researches of many sociologists - both male and female - have been hitherto.

10. Weller, L (1974) observed that sociology in Israel was influenced by Jewish sociologists of American origin and training.

11. Shogo Koyano (1976: 27) observed that the process of introducing American sociology in Japan was not necessarily straight forward. Although it was generally said that American sociology had stepped into the shoes of the German influence, the actual conditions of this change were rather complex. Japanese sociologists imported American method of research and sociological theory, through translations, mainly of American works. The general theory of Parsons has strongly affected Japanese sociologists particularily in its more abstract aspects.

(Yamagishi and Brinton, 1980: 192-207) state, 'The academic traditions of the United States have had a particularly strong impact on the development of the social sciences in Japan. Japanese sociology in the postwar period has been characterized by the overwhelming influence of American sociology, along with the increasing influence of Marxism. Empirical research methodology and quantitative techniques have been strongly advocated and widely accepted in the postwar years. Also reflecting trends in American sociology, the functionalist orientation gained in popularity during the sixties.'

12. The influence of American sociology on Finnish sociology definitely led to a great interest in theory and form on theory construction.

Allard (1977: 35) American textbooks were used in
Scandinavian countries. Theory, methods and research on
substantive areas in Scandinavian sociology were influenced by
American sociology.

Lochen (1982: 359) states: 'The ties between American and
Norwegian Sociology have been especially strong' - however, he
adds 'yet Norwegian sociology developed a separated and stubborn
identity of its own'.

4
BEYOND TRADITIONS: SOCIOLOGY OF INDIA

1. M. N. Srinivas, a former student of G.S. Ghurye states
(1973) that "Ghurye combined fruitfully the ethnological and
indological approaches and contributed to basing Sociology and
social anthropology in India on sound field work. From his chair
in Bombay, he directed a one man ethnographic survey of India, an
operation which was conducted with little or no financial
resources".

2. Srinivas (1973: 131) attributes the recent popularity of
sociology to the greatly increased exposure of Indian academics to
American universities during the last twenty-five years and to a
belated realization of the insufficiency of a purely economic
approach to development.

3. Srinivas refuses to make a distinction between social
anthropology and sociology in teaching and research because 'there
is a continuity in traditional India between tribes and castes and
any imported distinction between social anthropology and sociology
does violence to social reality'.

4. Desai (1981) brings to our attention that the dominant
approaches which shaped sociological studies in India have been
basically non-Marxist. He advocates the use of Marxist paradigm
as an alternative heuristic device for conducting fruitful and
relevant researches about the Indian society.

5. The bureaucrats, administrators, and politicians in India
have paid very little attention to social science research.
Weiner (1979) observes that "administrators do not pay much
attention to the social science research, they term it 'too
academic, too removed from social reality', while social
scientists find the government system 'is so vast, so complex, so
immobile' that any kind of change and innovation are difficult".

6. For an understanding of the influence of American support
to social research in India during the 1950-1970 period refer,
Chekki, Dan. A. - "American Support to Social Research: The Case

of India", Indian Journal of Social Research, 25: 1, April 1984, pp. 58-67.

7.   Sharma (1982) raises the question of relevance of Western sociological theories to reality in India in view of the fact that most of the existing sociological theories, apart from being Western in their origin, betray a tendency of Western ethnocentrism.   He demonstrates the dubious relevance of Western sociological theories for the third world mainly because of 1) historicity and relativity of social reality, 2) inadequacies of the existing theories and, 3) sociological universalism of the dominant society i.e. the U.S.A.   Furthermore, there have been various constraints on theory building in India.   These are: suprasocial intellectual tradition, colonial break and dependency, absence of an experience of intellectual suffering, and the context of under development.   Sharma concludes that sociological theories will only gain in generality by taking cognizance of social reality in the third world countries.   Paradoxically enough sociology is both a universal and culture-bound discipline.

5
THE QUEST FOR RELEVANCE AND NATIONALITY:
CANADIAN SOCIOLOGY

1.   Hiller (1982: 4-39) specifies four periods in the development of sociology in Canada.   They are the periods of European transferance (a time frame up to and including the First World War), environmental adaptation (from the First World War to the 1950s), disciplinary differentiation and specialization (essentially the 1960s) and consolidation (the 1970s).   Even though specific time boundaries for each of these periods are suggested, it is understood that they flow into one another and no rigid time frame is implied.

2.   'The development of Francophone and Anglophone societies in Canada proceeded at a different space.   Quebec sociology was less dependent on American sociology and was earlier characterized by a distinctive national style, sufficient to secure it a potent role in a changing Quebec society.   Anglophone society, on the other hand, struggled much more slowly to distinguish itself from the hegemony of American social science, and only of late has it indicated a viability that allows it to react to other national sociologies, rather than simply emulate them.'   (Forcese and Richer, 1975)

Hiller (1980) While Anglophone Sociology wrestled with the issue of fact-value distinction, Francophone sociology was rather reluctant to accept this distinction.

The Canadianization of sociology movement started in the late 1960s and in the early 1970s was a reaction to the dominance of

American sociological paradigms and faculty. It argued for greater Canadian content, employment of Canadian nationals, and development of theories, models, approaches that emanate from Canadian society and culture. This indigenization process led to greater sensitization in the discipline to society-specific characteristics and issues (Hiller, 1980, 270).

'The concern for a national disciplinary identity paralleled a general national concern for identity and differentiation. In the late 1970s and in the early 1980s Canadian sociologists have tended to adopt macro sociological perspectives using political economy, Neo Marxist and dependency theoretical orientations to analyse Canadian (and non-Canadian) contemporary issues and processes and have tried to demonstrate the relevance of such models for understanding Canadian society.' It is necessary to recognize that no single explanatory model is adequate even though all these models together seem to be relevant for understanding the growth of sociology in India and Canada.

3. Hiller (1980-81) demonstrates how research biography of S.D. Clark can be a useful tool to understand the development and change in Canadian sociology as it emerged from a dependent undifferentiated position to that of an autonomous highly differentiated discipline.

Harrison (1981) states that Clark's work represents the first articulation of a Canadian sociology. The opposition between its form and content makes it into something more than the medium through which the most salient elements of nationalism in Canadian sociology are brought together and understood.

4. 'The nationalist debate within Canadian Sociology during its most significant formative period reflects a preoccupation with external dominance' - Anglophone sociologists addressing the dominance of the U.S. and Francophone sociologists writing about English Canada's dominance on Quebec. The debate between universal and particular, national vs - international, and regional vs. national. 'The social science movement in Canada has reflected the realities, the paradoxes, and contradictions of Canada's development'....

5. It is recognized that much of Canadian Sociology has been derived from the dominant American tradition of functionalism which makes Canadian students of sociology often believe that they are learning a value-free universalistic perspective on society. In fact, however, they are often being subtly taught from the point of view of the dominant American paradigm. Furthermore, it is stated that a genuinely Canadian theoretical perspective on Sociology is simply too new to have well defined ideological and methodological camps beyond the dominant one. (McDaniel and Agger, 1983)

6. As regards the dominance of American Sociology in Canada, Clark (1976) maintained that Canadian sociologists should have knowledge about the evolution of Canadian Society, a sense of identification and sensitivity to the unique traits of Canadian society and he objected to the assumption that sociology was a universal science because it played down national societal differences. He viewed himself as 'faithful to the Toronto tradition of political economy' because his expectations of sociology were more humanistic less scientific and more historically interdisciplinary.

7. 'It is significant that the quest for a Canadian sociology paralleled developments in other countries for a sociology grounded in the national experience of a people for eg.: Sociologists in Australia and New Zealand influenced by paradigms dominant in American sociology, called for a genuine sociology of their own having distinct theoretical and substantive focus. Another parallel trend was the emergence of minority sociologies among particular groups (eg. black sociology, chicano sociology, and feminist sociology) who felt the need for development of sociological perspectives emerging from their own social experiences. In this sense, the quest for a Canadian Sociology represented one aspect of a widespread movement with in the discipline of both criticism of scientism and criticism of dominant perspectives within American Sociology. A second factor that provoked the Canadian Sociology movement into existence was the new wave of nationalism that began to be expressed in the late 1960s. (Hiller, 1982)

8. Canadianization - the two prominent themes were those of personnel and substantive content. The Canadian studies Committee was entrusted with the responsibility of stimulating the growth of Canadian content in sociological instruction.   The CSAA 1973 annual meetings passed a motion calling for a moratorium on the hiring of non-Canadians by Departments with less than fifty percent Canadians on their faculties.

During the second half of the 1970s a frequent plea was made for a more distinctive sociology, that is, a Canadian Sociology (rather than just a sociology of Canada or sociology in Canada) that developed theories or paradigms from phenomena characteristics of Canadian society. An economic dependency model with an emphasis on power relationships was frequently expressed as and antidote to more static conservative models. Furthermore, the reliance and posture of Francophone sociology of Quebec society was often inferred to be a more desirable position for anglophone sociologists for which to understand the Canadian experience.

There was a revival of the political economy approach - other approaches at the macro-level analysed ideologies or suggested the ultilization of the tools of phenomenology and ethnomethodology to understand the society.

In as much as the Canadian sociology movement stressed an attempt to develop a distinct themetical thrust(s), it represented a striving to engage in creative and independent reflection emerging from the intensive study of a particular society.

9. Loubser (1982), defines the process of 'indigenization' as the development of a national social science community that is self reliant, self sufficient and self directing, in other words autonomous and independent, with respect to all aspects of the vital functions of the community, including its ability to relate to other communities on an equal, reciprocal basis. It is stressed that indigenization of social science and a community of scholars can be attained if there is autonomy and independence from foreign domination in recruitment and training of members, content of teaching, conceptions of desirable subject matter, conceptual or theoretical models, methods and techniques, media for dissemination and discussion of results, research support and the incentive system. It is argued Loubser, (1982) that 'there could be no true internationalization of the social sciences without their indigenization over a wide range of countries and cultures in all regions of the world'. This is particularly true for the social sciences with their intimate relation to and intricate involvement in the social realities that they study'.

10. The Symons Report (1975), placed emphasis on 'To Know Ourselves' through Canadian studies and helped crystalize the matter of relating the social science to the Canadian milieu more distinctly. Similarly, in two science policy reports, the theme was also expressed that social science should not be imported.

11. The SSHRC program of thematic research is intended to establish a basis of knowledge on identified social needs or problems, support activities to help redress underdevelopment in specific areas in the humanities and social sciences. The report of the Social Science Federation of Canada Coordinating Committee on Strategic Grants recommended that thematic research must capitalize on existing strengths of the scholarly research efforts in the social sciences, if it is to play complementary role in relation to independent research.

12. Forcese and Richer (1982: 2-14) maintain that as late as 1975 the emergent Canadian sociology was still very much oriented to the hegemonous American discipline. In their view there was not yet a distinctively Canadian style or theme - a national sociology. It is stated that 'since then there have been indications that such a sociology is now imminent, if not already with us - one simple indicator is that Canadian sociologists are now unabashedly addressing Canadian social issues. Canadian

sociologists are defining their research themes and dealing with matters in their peculiarly Canadian manifestations. In sum, 'A simultaneous search for an understanding of the general, as well as the historically and nationally specific and unique, is the essence of a maturing Canadian sociology.

Committed to the notion of sociology as a social activity they are concerned with the societal context within which conceptual and research work are sustained by sociologists and their social background and life experiences. 'As in other areas of Canadian social life, an analysis of sociology in Canada would be incomplete without an explicit recognition of the influences from the South.'

Whyte (1982: 1-42) observes 'the fact that institutional sociology in Canada is of recent origin, and that it has taken shape during a period of challenge to external dominance and resurgence of internal nationalisms means that much of what sociology currently has to say about Canada is a reflection of both our societal condition and the state of the discipline in the Western world'.

13. Hedley and Warburton (1973: 299-319) while discussing the role of national courses, especially university courses bearing the label 'Canadian Society', in the teaching and development of sociology in Canada noted that increasing introduction of this kind of course reflected, among other factors, nationalistic reactions to American influences on various Canadian institutions. They argue that "the introduction of courses in Canadian Society in order to provide a truly Canadian contribution to sociology is merely the thin end of the wedge of sociological ethnocentrism", and in fact Warburton claims that the courses will have an undesirable ethnocentric impact on Sociology in Canada.

14. Whyte and Hiller provide a content analysis of Canadian sociology in the 1970s; identify the prominence of a political economy paradigm in Canadian sociology and the world system perspective.

6
CONCENSUS AND CONTROVERSY

1. In considering the role of the scientist in a classroom, Weber held that it was the task of the faculty member to illuminate rather than to exhort, to analyze rather than to prescribe, to delineate problems rather than to attempt to solve them.

'The sociologist is not a scientist in all roles. When called upon to serve as a social engineer, the sociologist is required to adopt value judgements and to decide upon goals. (Hauser, 1981: 62-64).

2. The two main traditions that dominate the debate: (i) The Hegalian-Marxian one, which stresses that social science plays a political role in the sense that it is part of the unfolding whole of society; and (ii) The Kantian-Weberian tradition, which emphasizes that social science, if properly handled, can be kept outside the political arena.

3. Refer, Appendix for data on sociologists in teaching, research, and applied settings.

4. Gray (1968) expresses a number of value judgments about the current practice of sociology and its dominant ideology. He maintains that sociologists who attempt to be value free do violence to their vocation by binding themselves to the values of others and sell their service to those with the most power and money as distinguished from those with the greatest need.

5. The Cacus of Unemployed/Underemployed Sociologists of the ASA declares (1984), "we are led to believe that privilege is hierarchically distributed based on an individualistic, meritocractic ideology. Yet we know that it is not only merit that determines rewards, but also class background, gender, race, luck and connections, and, for ourselves, time of getting our degrees. The problem is a social, not an individual one, and it calls for social, not individualistic solutions.

Overeducation is like over production: an irrational product of our irrational social system. Denying people who want to study the right to do so is like throwing milk into the harbor while babies starve.

Job creation in what is now being called "applied sociology" also has severe problems. While we strongly believe that sociology should be involved in society, and abhor the notion of an elitist ivory tower where ideas and research are separated from the concerns of people, we fear that applied sociology as it is being currently endorsed by ASA is easily subject to abuse. Jobs are much more likely to be created and controlled by institutions which commend wealth, such as private business firms, than they are by the poor and needy. Do we want to see sociology become a tool on behalf of priviledged classes in this society? Do we want to see sociologists working for the CIA? An unreflecting applied sociology can easily point us in this direction".

6. It is argued (Doris) that it is values, not science, that dictates (a) what we take to be socially relevant facts and (b) whether these 'facts' can successfully guide social policy.

7. McCartney (1984) examines the intellectual and political risks of setting priorities for social research in the context of recent budget cuts for social research. He concludes that sociologists must begin to discuss the objectives and strategies of funding social research, and seek ways of reducing dependency on federal funding.

8. While discussing the nature of professionalism in British sociology it is (Abrams, 1980) observed that if sociologists want to study society, and particularly if they want to change it, they have to accept obligations and commitments they might not otherwise choose.

Kaplan (Crawford and Rokka, 1976: 11-28) suggests that the role of the sociologist with respect to social change has been, and continues to be, largely counter-productive and ultimately counter-revolutionary.

9. "Sociology, politics, economics, law and education are moral sciences rather than natural sciences, and moral choices are not easy to justify solely by an appeal to facts. It is not the objective of the moral sciences to eliminate moral judgements from scholarly discourse, but only to sharpen the scholar's awareness of the nature and basis of his own moral judgment.

The training and equipment of a scholar enable him to discriminate between facts and values more rigorously and more systematically. It is not that scholarship and partisanship can never go together, but the scholar is more likely than the layman to be aware of his partisanship and to have a clearer sense of the cause for which he is a partisan. (Beteille, 1983: 7).

7
INTERNATIONAL AND NATIONAL SOCIOLOGIES

1. Demarath (1981) noted that foreign sociologists know far more about American sociology than American sociologies do about sociologies in other countries. He feels that as American sociology faces new challenges, it can ill afford to shun the experience of others.

APPENDIX

This appendix includes quantitative data on some selected aspects of the discipline of sociology, student enrolment, professional organizations etc. in the U.S.A., India, and Canada.

U.S.A.
TABLE 1
Membership in the American Sociological Association:
1906, 1981 and 1982

Category	1906	1981	1982
Full Member	-	9,183	9,415
Member Emeritus	-	413	406
Member Life	-		44
International Member	-	313	349
Associate Member	-	1,266	1,330
Associate Life	-		2
Associate Honorary	-		1
International Associate	-	603	622
Student Associate	-	1,660	1,930
Others	-	47	
TOTAL Membership	115*	13,485	14,099

*Only full-membership existed in 1906
Source: American Sociological Association
          Directory of Members, Washington
          D.C. 1982.

TABLE 2

Periodical Publications of the American Sociological Association

Journal	Frequency
American Sociological Review	Bimonthly
Official journal of the ASA; publishes articles on new trends and developments in theory and research.	
Contemporary Sociology	Bimonthly
A Journal of Reviews.	
Journal of Health and Social Behavior	Quarterly
Analysis of problems bearing on human health and illness.	
Sociology of Education	Quarterly
Concerned with research about education as a social institution and as a part of human social development	
Social Psychology Quarterly	Quarterly
Interdisciplinary journal of research and theory in social psychology.	
ASA Teaching Newsletter	
Footnotes	
A newsletter on activities and news of the profession, including official reports and proceedings of ASA groups.	Nine times/year
ASA Employment Bulletin	Monthly
Lists current positions available for Sociologists	

Source: American Sociological Association, (Washington, D.C.), 1984.

TABLE 3
ASA - Sponsored and other recent Publications

Sociological Methodology Annual	A History of the ASA: 1905-1980
Sociological Theory Semi-Annual	
Teaching Sociology Quarterly	Federal Funding Programs
Applied Sociology: Role & Activities of Sociologists in Diverse Settings	Guidelines to Initial Appointments
	Majoring in Sociology
Social Policy and Sociology	Embarking Upon a Career
Social Psychology: Sociological Perspectives	Mastering the Job Market
Annual Meeting Proceedings 1983	Index to the American Sociological Review
Biographical Directory of Members 1982	Index to the Journal of Health & Social Behavior
Directory of Departments of Sociology 1982	Presidential Series
	Rose Monograph Series
Guide to Graduate Departments of Sociology	Annual Review of Sociology
Publishing Options: An Author's Guide	

Source: American Sociological Association, Publications 1987

TABLE 4
Sections of the American Sociological Association: 1985

Aging, Sociology of	Methodology
Asia & Asian American	Organizations & Occupations
Collective Behaviour & Social Movements	Peace and War, Sociology of
Community	Political Economy of the World-System
Comparative Historical Sociology	Political Sociology
Criminology	Population, Sociology of
Education, Sociology of	Racial & Ethnic Minorities
Environmental Sociology	Sex & Gender, Sociology of
Family, Sociology of	Social Psychology
Marxist Sociology	Sociological Practice
Medical Sociology	Theoretical Sociology
	Undergraduate Education

Source: American Sociological Association, 80th Annual Meeting Program, August 1985

- 129 -

TABLE 5

Employment of M.A. and Ph.D. Sociologists: 1980 and 1990

Place of Employment	1980		1990*	
	Number Employed	% of Total	Number Employed	% of Total
In academia	14,529	69.5	14,570	64.8
In applied fields (total)	6,382	30.5	7,917	35.2
In government (total)	1,806	28.3	3,267	41.3
Federal	533	8.4	340	4.3
State	676	10.6	2,218	28.0
Local	597	9.4	709	9.0
In services and industries (total)	4,576	71.7	4,650	58.7
Educational services	1,855	29.0	1,533	19.4
Misc. professional services	722	11.3	925	11.7
Medical health services	702	11.0	1,111	14.0
Nonprofit organizations	676	10.6	607	7.7
Business management	293	4.6	400	5.1
Other services	87	1.4	73	0.9
Misc. industry	241	3.8	1	.0

*Estimated figures.
Percentages may not add to 100 due to rounding.
Adapted from R.W. Manderscheid and M. Greenwald, Supply and demand
of Sociologists in 1980.
Paper presented at the Annual Meeting of the American Sociological
Association,
September 6, 1982, San Francisco, Cal.: 1-16.

TABLE 6

Indian Sociological Society

Year	Life Membership
1952	107
1963	268
1966	314
1969	434
1971	500
1976	586
1978	705
1982	795

TABLE 7

Indian Sociological Society

Periodical Publication

Sociological Bulletin, published

twice per year

In 1971 the Journal's total

circulation was over 1000 copies

TABLE 8
Enrolment in Sociology (Including Social Work) at the Post-
Graduate and the Research Levels during the period from 1961-61
1981-82 - selected years only
(University Teaching Departments/University Colleges and
Affiliated Colleges Combined)

| Year | Level | Enrolment | |
		Post-Graduate	Research
1961-62		3490	169
1965-66		3165	217
1970-71		5247	315
1975-76		7420	460
1976-77		7316	491
1981-82		9215	957

Source: University Grants Commission, New Delhi.

TABLE 9
Out-Turn of Post-Graduates in Sociology (Including Social
Work) During the Period From 1966 to 1979 - Selected Years Only
(All Universities Combined)

Year	Out-Turn
1966	1642
1971	3178
1976	6981
1977	6183
1978	8633
1979	9254

Source: University Grants Commission, New Delhi.

TABLE 10
Out-Turn of Doctorates in Sociology (Including Social
Work) During the Period From 1950-51 to 1981-82 -
Selected Years Only

(All Universities Combined)

Year	Out-Turn
1950-51	5
1955-56	7
1960-61	14
1961-62	7
1965-66	19
1970-71	31
1975-76	43
1976-77	61
1977-78	81
1978-79	83
1979-80	62
1980-81	78
1981-82	101

Source: University Grants Commission, New Delhi

CANADA
TABLE 11
Total Receipts of the Canadian Social Science
Research Council, 1940-58

Rockefeller Foundation	$499,795
Ford Foundation	74,400
Carnegie Foundation	61,130
Subtotal	$636,325
Canadian Universities and	
Colleges	35,225
Private sources	47,300
Total	$718,850

Source: Mabel F. Timlin and Albert Faucher,
         The Social Sciences in Canada: Two
         Studies (Ottawa: Social Science
         Research Council of Canada 1968),
         table IX, p. 64.

TABLE 12

University growth in degrees awarded, 1960-61 to 1971-72

	No. of degrees awarded	% Bachelor degrees	% Master degrees
1960-61	22,440	88.2	9.9
1961-62	25,708	88.8	9.5
1962-63	28,345	88.0	9.7
1963-64	32,580	88.7	9.2
1964-65	37,489	88.2	9.5
1965-66	43,355	87.3	10.3
1966-67	49,721	86.9	10.6
1967-68	56,002	87.1	10.3
1968-69	63,465	86.2	11.1
1969-70	71,296	84.8	11.9
1970-71	79,219	84.7	12.2
1971-72	85,519	84.9	12.0

Source: Adapted from Statistics Canada, Catalogue 81-559, table 1, p. 14

TABLE 13

Full-time university professor for selected
disciplines and selected years

	Total faculty	Soc	Pol Sc	Econ	All Soc Sc	Phil	Civ Eng	Chem
1956-57	4,973	32	21	173	649	148	152	334
1960-61	6,454	61	54	216	942	217	194	402
1963-64	9,124	115	123	312	1,500	326	232	539
1967-68	16,703	300	328	594	3,386	505	353	838
1969-70	21,840	548	450	762	4,780	618	408	1,016
1971-72	26,959	829	684	860	6,124	697	440	1,051
1973-74	28,458	848	691	904	6,575	693	444	1,162
1975-76	30,784	903	712	960	7,239	666	349	896
1976-77	31,673	917	729	960	7,550	661	384	911

Source: Adapted from Statistics Canada, 'From the Sixties to the
Eighties: A Statistical Portrait of Canadian Higher
Education' (Paper prepared for the Twelfth Quinquennial
Congress of the Universities of the Commonwealth, 1978),
table 32

TABLE 14
Social Science doctoral degrees awarded in Canada
1956-57 to 1963-64, and doctoral candidates in
Canada, the United Kingdom, and the United
States, 1965-66, for selected disciplines

Discipline	Doctoral degrees awarded in Canada	Doctoral Candidates from Canada		
		Studying in Can.	Studying in U.K.	Studying in U.S.A.
Economics	28	57	37	93
Political economy	17	-	-	-
Political science	15	32	30	25
Anthropology	2	4	10	10
Sociology	1	11	6	38
History	51	72	53	*

*Unavailable
  Note: Political economy as a discipline is supplanted by
         individual disciplines during this period.
  Source: Compiled from Timlin and Faucher, The Social Sciences
         in Canada: Two Studies, pp. 44-9, tables III, IV, V,
         VII

TABLE 15 (a)
Percentage distribution of sociology faculty, social science
faculty, and all Canadan faculty by rank and selected years

Rank	1958-59			1963-64		
	Sociology faculty	All social science faculty	All faculty	Sociology faculty	All social science faculty	All faculty
Lecturers	10.0	18.2	17.2	16.7	19.9	19.8
Assistant professors	55.0	30.1	28.2	37.0	35.5	31.8
Associate professors	20.0	24.7	22.3	34.3	25.3	24.1
Professors	10.0	23.0	27.5	10.2	18.2	21.5
Others	5.0	3.9	4.7	1.9	1.2	2.8

Source: Compiled from Max von Zur Mehlen, "The Full-time Faculty
         of Canadian Universities, 1956/57 to 1974/75,"
         mimeographed (Statistics Canada 1977), table 19, pp.
         49-50.

TABLE 15 (b)
Percentage distribution of sociology faculty, social science
faculty, and all Canadan faculty by rank and selected years

Rank	1968-69 Sociology faculty	1968-69 All social science faculty	1968-69 All faculty	1973-74 Sociology faculty	1973-74 All social science faculty	1973-74 All faculty
Lecturers	24.8	15.6	16.7	18.2	12.0	22.1
Assistant professors	40.8	41.1	36.6	41.6	37.3	30.9
Associate professors	20.7	24.5	25.4	21.9	29.2	33.6
Professors	12.7	17.5	19.4	16.0	19.8	11.3
Others	1.0	1.3	1.8	2.2	1.7	2.1

Source: Compiled from Max von Zur Mehlen, "The Full-time Faculty
of Canadian Universities, 1956/57 to 1974/75,"
mimeographed (Statistics Canada 1977), table 19, pp.
49-50.

TABLE 16

Graduate degrees awarded in sociology by Canadian universities, 1961-75

	MA	MA	PHD	PHD
1960-61	11	*	0	*
1961-62	21	*	1	*
1962-63	19	*	0	*
1963-64	22	*	0	*
1964-65	32	*	0	*
1965-66	50	62	1	6
1966-67	73	74	1	4
1967-68	167	92	5	4
1968-69	170	151	5	7
1969-70	177	162	2	8
1970-71	192	178	12	8
1971-72	216	195	15	19
1972-73	250	208	23	26
1973-74	216	191	31	30
1974-75	*	184	*	39

*Unavailable or not compiled
Based on data gathered by Statistics Canada
Based on data gathered by the Canadian Association of Graduate Schools . and representative of degrees granted in the latter year mentioned (e.g 1965-66 = 1966)
Note: The data gathered by Statistics Canada and the Canadian Association of Graduate Schools are not exactly comparable because of differences in reporting periods, changes in definitions of disciplines by universities, and the lack of data for the earlier period in CAGS record.
Source: Compiled from data available in 'Degrees Awarded by Canadian Universities by Level and Discipline, during the Sixties and Early , Seventies' by Max von Zur Mehlen, mimeographed (Statistics Canada 1977) pp. 29, 39, 47, 57

BIBLIOGRAPHY

Abrams, P. et al. PRACTICE AND PROGRESS: BRITISH SOCIOLOGY, 1950-1980, London, Allen & Unwin, 1981.

Abrahamson, M. SOCIOLOGICAL THEORY: AN INTRODUCTION TO CONCEPTS, ISSUES, AND RESEARCH, Englewood Cliffs, N.J., Prentice-Hall, 1981.

Adams, B.N. COERCION AND CONSENSUS THEORIES: SOME UNRESOLVED ISSUES, American Journal of Sociology, LXXi, 1966, 714-717.

Ahmed, I. FOR A SOCIOLOGY OF INDIA, Contributions to Indian Sociology, 6, 1972.

American Sociological Association. CODE OF ETHICS, Washington, D.C., American Sociological Association, 1984.

American Sociological Association. REVISED CODE OF ETHICS, Footnotes, 10:3, pp. 9-10, 1982.

Anderson, A.A. et al. SOCIOLOGY IN CANADA: A DEVELOPMENTAL OVERVIEW, In Mohan and Martindale (eds.), Handbook of Contemporary Developments in World Sociology, pp. 159-171. Westport, CT., Greenwood, 1975.

Antonio, R. J. and P. Piran. THE POVERTY OF AMERICAN SOCIOLOGY: HISTORICITY AND EMPIRICISM, The 9th World Congress of Sociology, Uppsala, Sweden, August 14-19, 1978.

Anderson, C.H. TOWARD A NEW SOCIOLOGY: A CRITICAL VIEW, Homewood, ILL, The Dorsey Press, 1971.

Aron, R. MODERN SOCIETY AND SOCIOLOGY, in E.A. Tiryakian (ed.), The Phenomenon of Sociology, New York, Appleton, 1971.

Atal, Y. SOCIOLOGY IN THE INDIAN CAMPUS, in Gupta, G. R. (ed.), Main Currents in Indian Sociology, Vol. I, pp. 117-131, New Delhi, Vikas, 1976.

Bailey, F. G. FOR A SOCIOLOGY OF INDIA? Contributions to Indian Sociology, 3, 1959.

Baldock, C. V. and J. Lally. SOCIOLOGY IN AUSTRALIA AND NEW ZEALAND, in Mohan and Martindale (eds.), Handbook of Contemporary Developments in World Sociology, Westport, CT., Greenwood, 1975.

Baldock, C. V. and J. Lally. SOCIOLOGY IN AUSTRALIA AND NEW ZEALAND: THEORY AND METHODS, Westport, CT., Greenwood Press, 1974.

Bandyopadhyay, P. ONE SOCIOLOGY OR MANY: SOME ISSUES IN RADICAL SOCIOLOGY, Sociological Review, 19:1, 1971, pp 5-29.

Barnes, H. E. (ed.). AN INTRODUCTION TO THE HISTORY OF SOCIOLOGY, Chicago, University of Chicago Press, 1948.

Beattie, C. and S. Crysdale. SOCIOLOGY CANADA: READINGS, Toronto, Butterworth, 1974.

Becker, H. S. WHAT IS HAPPENING TO SOCIOLOGY?, Society, July/August, 1979, 19-24.

Becker, H. S. WHOSE SIDE ARE WE ON? Social Problems, 14, 1967, 239-247.

Becker, H. and H. E. Barnes. SOCIAL THOUGHT FROM LORE TO SCIENCE (3 vols.), 3rd Edition, New York, Dover, 1961.

Becker, H. S. and I. L. Horowitz. RADICAL POLITICS AND SOCIOLOGICAL RESEARCH: OBSERVATIONS ON METHODOLOGY AND IDEOLOGY, American Journal of Sociology, 78:1, 1972: 48-66.

Bell, D. THE SOCIAL SCIENCES SINCE THE SECOND WORLD WAR, New Brunswick, N.J., Transaction Books, 1982.

Ben-David, J. and R. Collins. SOCIAL FACTORS IN THE ORIGIN OF A NEW SCIENCE, American Sociological Review, 31, 1966: 451-466.

Berger, P. L. and T. Luckmann. THE SOCIAL CONSTRUCTION OF REALITY: A TREATISE IN THE SOCIOLOGY OF KNOWLEDGE, Garden City, N.Y., Doubleday, 1966.

Berger, P. L. INVITATION TO SOCIOLOGY, New York, Doubleday, 1963.

Berkowitz, S. D. MODELS AND MYTHS IN CANADIAN SOCIOLOGY, Scarborough, Butterworth, 1984.

Bernert, C. THE CAREER OF CAUSAL ANALYSIS IN AMERICAN SOCIOLOGY, British Journal of Sociology, 34:2, June 1983, 230-256.

Béteille, A. (ed.). EQUALITY AND INEQUALITY: THEORY AND PRACTICE, Delhi, Oxford University Press, 1983.

Bierstedt, R. THE SOCIAL ORDER, New York, McGraw-Hill, 1970.

Bierstedt, R. AMERICAN SOCIOLOGICAL THEORY: A CRITICAL HISTORY, New York, Academic Press, 1981.

Bierstedt, R. (ed.). A DESIGN FOR SOCIOLOGY: SCOPE, OBJECTIVES, AND METHOD, Philadelphia, The Annals, 1969.

Bierstedt, R.   SOCIOLOGY AND HUMANE LEARNING, American
   Sociological Review, 25, 1960.

Bierstedt, R.   TOYNBEE AND SOCIOLOGY, British Journal of
   Sociology, 10:2, 1959, 95-104.

Birnbaum, N.   'FOREWORD', in R. W. Friedrichs, Sociology of
   Sociology, New York, Free Press, 1970.

Blackburn, R. (ed.).   IDEOLOGY IN SOCIAL SCIENCE: READINGS IN
   CRITICAL SOCIAL THEORY, London, Fontana, 1972.

Blau, P.M.   EXCHANGE AND POWER IN SOCIAL LIFE, New York, Wiley,
   1964.

Blumer, H.   SYMBOLIC INTERACTIONISM: PERSPECTIVE AND METHOD,
   Englewood Cliffs, N.J., Prentice-Hall, 1969.

Boalt, G.   THE SOCIOLOGY OF RESEARCH, Southern Illinois University
   Press, 1969.

Bogardus, E. S.   TWENTY-FIVE YEARS OF AMERICAN SOCIOLOGY,
   Sociology and Social Research, 57:2, January 1973, 145-152.

Bottomore, T. et al (eds.).   SOCIOLOGY: THE STATE OF THE ART,
   London and Beverly Hills, Sage Publications, 1982.

Bottomore, T. and R. Nisbet (eds.).   A HISTORY OF SOCIOLOGICAL
   ANALYSIS, New York, Basic Books, 1978.

Bottomore, T. B.   COMPETING PARADIGMS IN MACROSOCIOLOGY, Palo
   Alto, Annual Review of Sociology, 1975.

Bottomore, T. B.   SOCIOLOGY IN INDIA, British Journal of
   Sociology, 13, 1962.

Boudon, R.   THE CRISIS IN SOCIOLOGY: PROBLEMS OF SOCIOLOGICAL
   EPISTEMOLOGY, New York, Columbia University Press, 1980.

Bramson, L.   THE POLITICAL CONTEXT OF SOCIOLOGY, Princeton,
   Princeton University Press, 1961.

Brooks, H.   THE EFFECT OF SPONSORSHIP UPON SOCIAL SCIENCE
   RESEARCH, Items, 37:2-3, Sept., 1983, pp. 43-46.

Brown, J. S. and B. G. Gilmartin.   SOCIOLOGY TODAY: LACUNAE,
   EMPHASIS AND SURFEITS, American Sociologist, 4, 1969.

Brym, R. J. ANGLO-CANADIAN SOCIOLOGY, Current Sociology, 34:1,
   1986.

Bulmer, M. (ed.).   SOCIAL RESEARCH ETHICS: AN EXAMINATION OF THE
     MERITS OF COVERT PARTICIPANT OBSERVATION, New York, Holmes and
     Meier, 1982.

Burr, W. R. et al (eds.). CONTEMPORARY THEORIES ABOUT THE FAMILY,
     VOL.II., New York, Free Press, 1979.
Canadian Sociology and Anthropology Association.   CODE OF
     PROFESSIONAL ETHICS, CSAA Bulletin, April 1979.

Castells, M.   THEORY AND IDEOLOGY IN URBAN SOCIOLOGY, in C. G.
     Pickvance (eds.), Urban Sociology: Critical Essays, pp. 60-84,
     London, Tavistock, 1976.

Chekki, D. A.   AMERICAN SUPPORT TO SOCIAL RESEARCH: THE CASE OF
     I N D I A ,   Indian Journal of Social Research, 25:1, April 1984,
     58-67.

Chekki, D. A.   THE SOCIOLOGY OF CONTEMPORARY INDIA, New Delhi,
     Sterling, and Columbia, Mo., South Asia Books, 1978.

Chekki, D. A.   THE SOCIAL SYSTEM AND CULTURE OF MODERN INDIA, New
     York and London, Garland Publishers, 1975.

Clark, S. D.   SOCIOLOGY IN CANADA: AN HISTORICAL OVERVIEW,
     Canadian Journal of Sociology, 1:2, 1975, 225-234.

Clement, W.   MACRO-SOCIOLOGICAL APPROACHES TOWARD A CANADIAN
     SOCIOLOGY, Alternate Routes, 1977, 1:1, 1-37.

Clinard, M. B. and J. W. Elder. SOCIOLOGY IN INDIA: A STUDY IN
     THE SOCIOLOGY OF KNOWLEDGE, American Sociological Review, 30,
     1965, 581-587.

Coburn, D. SOCIOLOGY AND SOCIOLOGISTS IN CANADA: PROBLEMS AND
     PROSPECTS, in J. J. Loubser (ed.)., The Future of Sociology in
     Canada, pp. 37-59.   Montreal, Canadian Sociology and
     Anthropology Association, 1970.

Collins, R. CONFLICT SOCIOLOGY, New York, Academic Press, 1975.

Conner, D. M. and J. E. Curtis. SOCIOLOGY AND ANTHROPOLOGY IN
     C A N A D A , Montreal, Canadian Sociology and Anthropology
     Association, 1970.

Coser, L. A.   SOCIOLOGICAL THEORY FROM THE CHICAGO DOMINANCE TO
     1965, Palo Alto, Annual Review of Sociology, 1976.

Coser, L. A.   TWO METHODS IN SEARCH OF A SUBSTANCE, American
     Sociological Review, 40:6, 1975, pp. 691-700.

Coser, L. A. MASTERS OF SOCIOLOGICAL THOUGHT, New York, Harcourt, 1971.

Crawford, E. and S. Rokkan (eds.). SOCIOLOGICAL PRAXIS: CURRENT ROLES AND SETTINGS, London, Sage Publications, 1976.

Crook, R. K. N. TEACHING AND LEARNING SOCIOLOGY, in Forces, D. and S. Richer (eds.), Issues in Canadian Society, pp. 467-498. Scarborough, Prentice-Hall of Canada, 1975.

Cunningham, F. OBJECTIVITY IN SOCIAL SCIENCE, Toronto, University of Toronto Press, 1975.

Curtis, J. E. and J. W. Petras (eds.). THE SOCIOLOGY OF KNOWLEDGE, New York, Praeger, 1970.

Damle, Y. B. FOR A THEORY OF INDIAN SOCIOLOGY in Sociology in India. Agra, Institute of Social Sciences, Agra University, 1965, 32-52.

Davis, A. K. SOME FAILINGS OF ANGLOPHONE ACADEMIC SOCIOLOGY IN CANADA, in J. G. Loubser (ed.), The Future of Sociology in Canada, Montreal, Canadian Sociology and Anthropology Association, 1970.

Das, M. S. (ed.) CONTEMPORARY SOCIOLOGY IN THE U.S., New Delhi, Vikas, 1983.

Demarath III, N. J. et al. SOCIAL POLICY AND SOCIOLOGY, New York, Academic Press, 1975.

Demarath III, N. J. SACRED AND PROFANE IN SOCIOLOGY AND SOCIAL POLICY: COMPARATIVE NOTES ON BRITAIN AND THE U.S., American Sociologist, 16:3, 1981, 136-147.

Denzin, N. K. WHO LEADS: SOCIOLOGY OR SOCIETY?, American Sociologist, 5, 1970, 125-127.

Desai, A. R. RELEVANCE OF THE MARXIST APPROACH TO THE STUDY OF INDIAN SOCIETY, Sociological Bulletin, 30:1, March, 1981, 1-20.

Desai, I. P. THE CRAFT OF SOCIOLOGY AND OTHER ESSAYS, Delhi, Ajanta Publications, 1981.

Desai, I. P. CRAFT OF SOCIOLOGY IN INDIA: AN AUTOBIOGRAPHICAL PERSPECTIVE, Economic and Political Weekly, February 7, 1981, 197-204; February 14, 1981, 246-252.

Dube, S. C. INDIAN SOCIOLOGY AT THE TURNING POINT, Sociological Bulletin, 26:1, 1977, 1-13.

Dube, S. C. SOCIAL ANTHROPOLOGY IN INDIA, in T. Madan and G. Saran (eds.), Indian Anthropology. Bombay, Asia, 1962.

Dumont, L. and D. Pocock. FOR A SOCIOLOGY OF INDIA, Contributions to Indian Sociology, I, 1957, 7-22.

Dynes, R. R. SOCIOLOGY AS A RELIGIOUS MOVEMENT: THOUGHTS ON ITS INSTITUTIONALIZATION IN THE UNITED STATES, American Sociologist, 9:4, 1974, 169-176.

Eckberg, D. L. and L. Hill. THE PARADIGM CONCEPT AND SOCIOLOGY: A CRITICAL REVIEW, American Sociological Review, 44, 1979, 925-937.

Eichler, M. AND THE WORK NEVER ENDS: FEMINIST CONTRIBUTIONS, Canadian Review of Sociology and Anthropology, 22:5, December, 1985, 609-644.

Eisenstadt, S. N. THE SCHOOLS OF SOCIOLOGY, American Behavioral Scientist, 24:3, Jan.-Feb., 1981, 329-344.

Eisenstadt, S. N. THE FORM OF SOCIOLOGY: PARADIGMS AND CRISES, New York, Wiley, 1976.

Elkin, F. SOCIOLOGY IN CANADA, in J. S. Roucek (ed.), Contemporary Sociology, New York, Philosophical Library, 1958.

Faris, R. E. L. AMERICAN SOCIOLOGY, in G. Gurvitch and W. E. Moore (eds.), Twentieth Century Sociology, New York, The Philosophical Library, 1945.

Felt, L. NATIONALISM AND THE POSSIBILITY OF A RELEVANT ANGLO-CANADIAN SOCIOLOGY, Canadian Journal of Sociology, 1975, 1:377-385.

Fichter, J. H. SOCIOLOGY FOR OUR TIMES, Social Forces, 62:3, March 1984, pp.573-584.

Filmer, P. et al. NEW DIRECTIONS IN SOCIOLOGICAL THEORY, Cambridge, MIT Press, 1972.

Flacks, R. and G. Turkel. RADICAL SOCIOLOGY, Palo Alto, Annual Review of Sociology, 1978.

Forcese, D. and S. Richer (eds.). SOCIAL ISSUES: SOCIOLOGICAL VIEWS OF CANADA, Scarborough, Prentice-Hall Canada, 1982.

Forcese, D. and S. Richer (eds.). ISSUES IN CANADIAN SOCIETY, Scarborough, Prentice-Hall, 1975, 449-466.

Freeman, H. E. et al. APPLIED SOCIOLOGY: ROLES AND ACTIVITIES OF SOCIOLOGISTS IN DIVERSE SETTINGS, San Francisco, Jossey-Bass, 1983.

Friedrichs, R. W. ETHICS IN SOCIAL RESEARCH - A REVIEW ESSAY, Sociological Quarterly, 24, Summer 1983, 453-462.

Friedrichs, R. W. EPISTEMOLOGICAL FOUNDATIONS FOR A SOCIOLOGICAL ETHIC, American Sociologist, 5, 1970, 138-141.

Friederichs, R. W. SOCIOLOGY OF SOCIOLOGY, New York, The Free Press, 1970.

Friedrichs, R. W. CHOICE AND COMMITMENT IN SOCIAL RESEARCH, American Sociologist, 3, 1968, 8-11.

Frumkin, R. M. CONTEMPORARY SOCIOLOGY IN THE UNITED STATES, in Mohan and Martindale (eds.), Handbook of Contemporary Developments in World Sociology, Westport, CT., Greenwood, 1975, pp. 131-157.

Fuhrman, E. IS THIS SCIENCE AND/OR INTERNATIONAL? Society, July/August 1985, pp. 20-22.

Fuhrman, E. ALVIN GOULDNER AND THE SOCIOLOGY OF KNOWLEDGE: THREE SIGNIFICANT PROBLEM SHIFTS, Sociological Quarterly, 25:3, 1984, 287-300.

Fuhrman, E. R. THE SOCIOLOGY OF KNOWLEDGE IN AMERICA, 1883-1915, Charlottesville, Va., University Press of Virginia, 1980.

Fuhrman, E. R. CRITICAL THEORY AND THE HISTORY OF SOCIAL THEORY, Humboldt Journal of Social Relations 5:2, 1978, 1-25.

Furfey, P. H. SOCIOLOGICAL SCIENCE AND THE PROBLEM OF VALUES, in L. Gross (ed.), Symposium on Sociological Theory, Evanston, Row, Peterson, 509-530, 1959.

Gamson, W. SOCIOLOGY'S CHILDREN OF AFFLUENCE, American Sociologist, 3, 1968, 286-288.

Ganguli, B. N. IDEOLOGIES AND THE SOCIAL SCIENCES, Atlantic Highlands, N.J., Humanities Press, 1975.

Gardezi, H. N. CONTEMPORARY SOCIOLOGY IN PAKISTAN AND BANGLADESH, in Mohan and Martindale (eds.), Handbook of Contemporary Developments in World Sociology, Westport, CT., Greenwood, 1975.

Garfinkel, H. STUDIES IN ETHNOMETHODOLOGY, Englewood Cliffs, N.J., Prentice-Hall, 1967.

Gibbs, J. P. THE ELITES CAN DO WITHOUT US, American Sociologist, 14, 1979, 79-85.

Glass, J. F. THE HUMANISTIC CHALLENGE TO SOCIOLOGY, in Wells A. (ed.), Contemporary Sociological Theories, Santa Monica, Goodyear, 1978, 364-372.

Glasser, E. M. et al. PUTTING KNOWLEDGE TO USE, San Francisco, Jossey-Bass, 1983.

Glenn, N. D. and D. Weiner. SOME TRENDS IN THE SOCIAL ORIGINS OF AMERICAN SOCIOLOGISTS, American Sociologist, 4:4, 1969, 291-302.

Gore, M. S. SOCIAL POLICY AND THE SOCIOLOGIST, Indian Journal of Social Research, 25:1, 1984, pp. 85-93.

Gouldner, A. THE DIALECTIC OF IDEOLOGY AND TECHNOLOGY, New York, Seabury, 1976.

Gouldner, A. FOR SOCIOLOGY: RENEWAL AND CRITIQUE IN SOCIOLOGY TODAY, New York, Basre Books, 1973.

Gouldner, A. THE COMING CRISIS OF WESTERN SOCIOLOGY, New York, Avon, 1971.

Gouldner, A. W. THE SOCIOLOGIST AS PARTISAN: SOCIOLOGY AND THE WELFARE STATE, The American Sociologist, 3, 1968, 103-116.

Gouldner, A. W. ANTI-MINOTAUR: THE MYTH OF A VALUE-FREE SOCIOLOGY, Social Problems, 9:3, 1962, 199-213.

Gove, W. R. SHOULD THE SOCIOLOGY PROFESSION TAKE MORAL STANDS ON POLITICAL ISSUES?, American Sociologist, 5:3, 1970, 221-223.

Gray, D. J. AMERICAN SOCIOLOGY: PLIGHT AND PROMISE, American Sociologist, 14, 1979, 35-42.

Gray, D. VALUE-FREE SOCIOLOGY: A DOCTRINE OF HYPOCRISY AND IRRESPONSIBILITY, Sociological Quarterly, 9, 1968, 176-185.

Greenaway, W. K. CRIME AND CLASS: UNEQUAL BEFORE THE LAW, in Harp and Hofley (eds.), Structured Inequality in Canada, pp. 247-265, Scarborough, Prentice-Hall of Canada, 1980.
Guinsburg, T. N. and G. L. Reuber (eds.), PERSPECTIVES ON THE SOCIAL SCIENCES IN CANADA, Toronto, University of Toronto Press, 1974.

Gupta, R. G. (ed.). MAIN CURRENTS IN INDIAN SOCIOLOGY, Vol.I, Delhi, Vikas, 1976.

Gurney, P. J. HISTORICAL ORIGINS OF IDEOLOGICAL DENIAL: THE CASE OF MARX IN AMERICAN SOCIOLOGY, American Sociologist, 16:3, 1981, 196-201.

Gurstein, M. TOWARDS THE NATIONALIZATION OF CANADIAN SOCIOLOGY, Journal of Canadian Studies, 1972, 7:3, 50-58.

Halmos, P. (ed.). THE SOCIOLOGY OF SOCIOLOGY, Keele, University of Keele, The Sociological Review Monograph No. 16, 1970.

Hamnett, M., D. J. Porter, A. Singh and K. Kumar. ETHICS, POLITICS AND INTERNATIONAL SOCIAL SCIENCE RESEARCH: FROM CRITIQUE TO PRAXIS, Honolulu, East-West Center, University of Hawaii Press, 1984.

Harrison, D. THE LIMITS OF LIBERALISM: THE MAKING OF CANADIAN SOCIOLOGY, Montreal, Black Rose Books, 1982.

Harvey, Lee. THE USE AND ABUSE OF KUHNIAN PARADIGMS IN THE SOCIOLOGY OF KNOWLEDGE, Sociology (BSA) 16:1, Feb., 1982, 85-101.

Hauser, P. M. SOCIOLOGY'S PROGRESS TOWARD SCIENCE, American Sociologist, 16, 1981, 62-64.

Hedley, R. A. and T. R. Warburton. THE ROLE OF NATIONAL COURSES IN THE TEACHING AND DEVELOPMENT OF SOCIOLOGY: THE CANADIAN CASE, Sociological Review, 21:7, 1973, pp. 299-319.

Heeren, J. W. and B. L. Poss. BECOMING A REALITY CONSTRUCTIONIST: AN UNEXPLORED AREA OF THE SOCIOLOGY OF SOCIOLOGY, American Sociologist, 6:2, 1971, 158-160.

Hiller, H. H. SOCIETY AND CHANGE: S.D. CLARK AND THE DEVELOPMENT OF CANADIAN SOCIOLOGY, Toronto, University of Toronto Press, 1982.

Hiller, H. H. NATIONALITY, RELEVANCE, AND ETHNOCENTRISM: AN ESSAY IN THE SOCIOLOGY OF CANADIAN BOOK PUBLISHING, Social Forces, 59:4, June 1981, 1297-1307.

Hiller, H. H. RESEARCH BIOGRAPHY AND DISCIPLINARY DEVELOPMENT: S.D. CLARK AND CANADIAN SOCIOLOGY, Journal of the History of Sociology, 3:1, 1980-81, 67-86.

Hiller, H. H. PARADIGMATIC SHIFTS, INDIGENIZATION, AND THE DEVELOPMENT OF SOCIOLOGY IN CANADA, Journal of the History of the Behavioral Sciences, 16, 1980, 263-274.

Hiller, H. H. THE CANADIAN SOCIOLOGY MOVEMENT: ANALYSIS AND ASSESSMENT, Canadian Journal of Sociology, 4:2, 1979, 125-150.

Hiller, H. H. UNIVERSALITY OF SCIENCE AND THE QUESTION OF NATIONAL SOCIOLOGIES, American Sociologist, 14, 1979, 124-135.

Hinkle, R. C. FOUNDING THEORY OF AMERICAN SOCIOLOGY, 1881-1915, Boston, Routledge and Kegan Print, 1980.

Hinkle, R. C. and G. J. Hinkle. THE DEVELOPMENT OF MODERN SOCIOLOGY: IT'S NATURE AND GROWTH IN THE UNITED STATES, New York, Random, 1954.

Hofley, J. R. JOHN PORTER: HIS ANALYSIS OF CLASS AND HIS CONTRIBUTION TO CANADIAN SOCIOLOGY, Canadian Review of Sociology and Anthropology, 18:5, December 1981, 595-606.

Hofley, J. R. PROBLEMS AND PERSPECTIVES IN THE STUDY OF POVERTY in Harp, J. and J. R. Hofley (eds.), Poverty in Canada, pp. 101-115, Scarborough, Prentice-Hall of Canada, 1971.

Hofstee, E. W. THE RELATIONS BETWEEN SOCIOLOGY AND POLICY, Sociologia Ruralis, 10:4, 1970, 331-345.

Hollander, P. COMPARATIVE SOCIOLOGY IN THE U.S., AND WHY THERE IS SO LITTLE OF IT?, Current Perspectives in Social Theory, Volume II, pp. 21-30, Greenwich, Jai Press, 1981.

Homans, G. C. SOCIAL BEHAVIOR: ITS ELEMENTARY FORMS, New York, Harcourt, 1974.

Homans, G.C. FIFTY YEARS OF SOCIOLOGY, Annual Review of Sociology, vol. 12, 1986.

Horowitz, I. PROFESSING SOCIOLOGY, Chicago, Aldine, 1968.

Horowitz, I. L. MAINLINERS AND MARGINALS: THE HUMAN SHAPE OF SOCIOLOGICAL THEORY, in L. Gross (ed.), Sociological Theory: Inquiries and Paradigms, New York, Harper and Row, 1967.

Horton, J. ORDER AND CONFLICT THEORIES OF SOCIAL PROBLEMS AS COMPETING IDEOLOGIES, American Journal of Sociology, LXXI, 1966, 701-13.

Hughes, E. ETHNOCENTRIC SOCIOLOGY, Social Forces, 40, 1961, 1-4.

Indian Council of Social Science Research. A SURVEY OF RESEARCH IN SOCIOLOGY AND SOCIAL ANTHROPOLOGY, 3 Vols., Bombay, Popular Prakashan, 1972, 1974.

Indra Deva. POSSIBILITY OF AN 'INDIAN SOCIOLOGY', in Unnithan et al (eds.) Sociology for India, New Delhi, Prentice-Hall, 1967.

Ishwaran, K. THE SOCIOLOGY OF SOCIOLOGY, International Journal of Comparative Sociology, 6, 1965, 278-284.

Jackson, J.D. (ed.), THE CANADIAN REVIEW OF SOCIOLOGY AND ANTHROPOLOGY, Special Issue on the State of the Art and New Directions, Volume I, Sociology in Anglophone Canada, 22:5 December 1985.

Janowitz, M. PROFESSIONALIZATION OF SOCIOLOGY, American Journal of Sociology, 78:1, 1972: 105-135.

Janowitz, M. POLITICAL CONFLICT: ESSAYS IN POLITICAL SOCIOLOGY, Chicago, Quadrangle Books, 1970.

Jarvie, I. C. NATIONALISM AND THE SOCIAL SCIENCES, Canadian Journal of Sociology, 1:4, 1976, pp. 515-528.

Kantowsky, D. A CRITICAL NOTE ON THE SOCIOLOGY OF DEVELOPING COUNTRIES. Contributions to Indian Sociology, 3, 1969.

Kelman, H. C. THE RELEVANCE OF SOCIAL RESEARCH TO SOCIAL ISSUES: PROMISES AND PITFALLS, in Halmos, P. (ed.), The Sociology of Sociology, Keele, University of Keele, 1970.

Keyfitz, N. SOCIOLOGY AND CANADIAN SOCIETY, in Perspectives on the Social Sciences, eds., Guinsberg and Reuber, Toronto, University of Toronto Press, 1974.

Kinloch, G. C. THE DEVELOPMENT OF AMERICAN SOCIOLOGY AS REFLECTED IN JOURNAL DEBATES, International Journal of Contemporary Sociology, 21:1-2, 1984, pp. 65-81.

Kinloch, G. C. IDEOLOGY AND CONTEMPORARY SOCIOLOGICAL THEORY, Englewood Cliffs, N.J., Prentice-Hall, 1981.

Kinloch, G. C. PROFESSIONAL SOCIOLOGY AS THE BASIS OF SOCIETAL INTEGRATION: A STUDY OF PRESIDENTIAL ADDRESSES, American Sociologist, 16, 1981, 2-13.

Knorr-Cetina, K. and Cicourel, A. V. ADVANCES IN SOCIAL THEORY AND METHODOLOGY: AN INTEGRTION OF MICRO - AND MACRO - SOCIOLOGY, Boston, Routledge and Kegan Paul, 1981.

Kolaja, J. (ed.). SCANDINAVIAN SOCIOLOGY, Current Sociology, 25:1, 1977.

Koyano, S. (ed.). SOCIOLOGICAL STUDIES IN JAPAN, Current Sociology, 24:1, 1976.

Krausz, E. SOCIOLOGY IN BRITAIN, New York Columbia University Press, 1969.

Kuhn, T. S.   THE STRUCTURE OF SCIENTIFIC REVOLUTIONS, Chicago, University of Chicago Press, 1970.

Kumar, K. and S. Raju.   DEPENDENCE IN SOCIOLOGY: AN EMPIRICAL STUDY OF ASIAN COUNTRIES, South East Asian Journal of Social Science,   9:1-2, 1981, pp. 100-122.

Lambert, R. D. and J. Curtis.   NATIONALITY AND PROFESSIONAL ACTIVITY CORRELATES AMONG SOCIAL SCIENTISTS, Canadian Review of Sociology   and Anthropology, 10, 1973: 62-80.

Lamy, P.   THE GLOBALIZATION OF AMERICAN SOCIOLOGY: EXCELLENCE OR IMPERIALISM, American Sociologist, 11, 1976, 104-114.

Lantz, H. R.   CONTINUITIES AND DISCONTINUITIES IN AMERICAN SOCIOLOGY, Sociological Quarterly, 25:4, 1984, 581-596.

Lazarsfeld, P.F.   MAIN TRENDS IN SOCIOLOGY, New York, Harper, 1970.

Lee, A. M.   SOCIOLOGY FOR WHOM?   New York, Oxford University Press, 1978.

Lee, G. R.   THE UTILITY OF CROSS-CULTURAL DATA: POTENTIALS AND LIMITATIONS FOR FAMILY SOCIOLOGY, Journal of Family Issues 5:4, December 1984, 519-41.

Lemke, J., D. Shevach and R. H. Wells.   THE HUMANISM - POSITIVISM DEBATE IN SOCIOLOGY: A COMMENT ON TOBBETS'S RECONSIDERATION, Sociological Inquiry, 54:1, 1984, 89-97.

Lengermann, P. M.   DEFINITIONS OF SOCIOLOGY: A HISTORICAL APPROACH, Columbus, Ohio, C. E. Merrill Publishing Co., 1974.

Levi-Strauss, C.   STRUCTURAL ANTHROPOLOGY, New York, Anchor Books, 1967.

Lipset, S. M.   and E. C. Ladd.   THE POLITICS OF AMERICAN SOCIOLOGISTS, American Journal of Sociology, 78, 1972, 67-104.

Lipset, S. M.   THE VALUE PATTERNS OF DEMOCRACY: A CASE STUDY IN COMPARATIVE ANALYSIS, American Sociological Review, 28, 1963, 515-531.

Lipset, S. M.   THE FIRST NEW NATION, New York, Basic, 1963.

Lipset, S. M. and N. J. Smelser (eds.), SOCIOLOGY: THE PROGRESS OF   A DECADE, Englewood Cliffs, N.J., Prentice-Hall, 1961.

Loubser, J. J.   THE NEED FOR THE INDIGENIZATION OF THE SOCIAL
  SCIENCES, paper presented at the 10th World Congress of
  Sociology, Mexico City, Mexico, August, 1982.

Loubser, J. J. (ed.).   THE FUTURE OF SOCIOLOGY IN CANADA,
  Montreal, Canadian Sociology and Anthropology Association,
  1970.

Luhmann, N.   INSISTENCE ON SYSTEMS THEORY: PERSPECTIVES FROM
  GERMANY - AN ESSAY, Social Forces, 61:4, June 1983, 987-998.

Lynd, R. KNOWLEDGE FOR WHAT?,   Princeton, Princeton University
  Press, 1939.

Mack. R.   THEORETICAL AND SUBSTANTIVE BIASES IN SOCIOLOGICAL
  RESEARCH, in M. Sherif and C. W. Sherif (eds.,),
  Interdisciplinary Relationships in the Social Sciences, pp.
  52-64, Chicago, Aldine, 1969.

Mackie, M.   SOCIOLOGY, ACADEMIA, AND THE COMMUNITY: MALIGNED
  WITHIN, INVISIBLE WITHOUT?,   Canadian Journal of Sociology,
  1:2, 1975, 203-221.

MacRae, D.   A DILEMMA OF SOCIOLOGY: SCIENCE VERSUS POLICY,
  American Sociologist, 6, 1971, 2-7.

Madan, T. N. INDIGENISATION OF SOCIAL SCIENCES, ICSSR Newsletter,
  April-September, 1979.

Madan, T. N.   POLITICAL PRESSURES AND ETHICAL CONSTRAINTS UPON
  INDIAN SOCIOLOGISTS, in Ethics, Politics, and Social Research,
  ed. G. Sjoberg, Cambridge, Mass., Schenkman, 1967.

Madan, T. N.   FOR A SOCIOLOGY OF INDIA: SOME CLARIFICATIONS,
  Contributions to Indian Sociology, 1, N.S. 1967.

Madan, T. N.   FOR A SOCIOLOGY OF INDIA, Contributions to Indian
  Sociology, 9, 1966.

Madge, J. THE ORIGINS OF SCIENTIFIC SOCIOLOGY, New York, The Free
  Press, 1968.

Mandelbaum, D. SOCIETY IN INDIA, 2 Vols., Berkeley, University of
  California Press, 1970.

Mannheim, K.   IDEOLOGY AND UTOPIA, New York, Harcourt, Brace and
  World, 1936.

Mannheim, K.   ESSAYS ON THE SOCIOLOGY OF KNOWLEDGE, London,
  Routledge and Kegan Paul, 1952.

Marchak, P. CANADAIN POLITICAL ECONOMY, Canadian Review of Sociology and Anthropology, 22:5, December, 1985, 673-709.

Markovic, M. ETHICS OF A CRITICAL SOCIAL SCIENCE, International Social Science Journal, 24:4, 1972.

Marsh, R. M. COMPARATIVE SOCIOLOGY, New York, Harcourt, 1967.

Martindale, D. and R. P. Mohan. SOME PROBLEM AREAS OF PROFESSIONAL SOCIAL SCIENCE, International Journal of Comtemporary Sociology, 16:1-2, 1979, 2-32.

Martindale, D. IDEOLOGIES, PARADIGMS, AND THEORIES, in Snizek, W. E. et al (eds.) Contemporary Issues in Theory and Method, Westport, CT., Greenwood, 1979.

Martindale, D. THE ROMANCE OF A PROFESSION: A CASE HISTORY IN THE SOCIOLOGY OF SOCIOLOGY, St. Paul, MN., Windflower, 1976.

Martindale, D. SOCIOLOGICAL THEORY AND THE PROBLEM OF VALUES, Columbus, Merrit, 1974.

Marx, K. and F. Engels. GERMAN IDEOLOGY (ed. by R. Pascal), New York, International Publishers, 1963.

McCartney, J. L. SETTING PRIORITIES FOR RESEARCH: NEW POLICIES FOR THE SOCIAL SCIENCES, Sociological Quarterly, 25:4, 1984, 437-455.

McCartney, J. L. ON BEING SCIENTIFIC: CHANGING STYLES OF PRESENTATION OF SOCIOLOGICAL RESEARCH, American Sociologist, 4:47-50, 1970.

McDaniel, S. A. and B. Agger. SOCIAL PROBLEMS THROUGH CONFLICT AND ORDER, Don Mills, Addison-Wesley, 1982.

Merton, R. K. and M. W. Riley. SOCIOLOGICAL TRADITION FROM GENERATION TO GENERATION, Norwood, N.J., Ablex, 1980.

Merton, R. K. INSIDERS AND OUTSIDERS: A CHAPTER IN THE SOCIOLOGY OF KNOWLEDGE, American Journal of Sociology, 78:1, 1972, 9-47.

Merton, R. K. SOCIAL THEORY AND SOCIAL STRUCTURE, New York, The Free Press, 1968.

Merton, R. K. et al (eds.). SOCIOLOGY TODAY: PROBLEMS AND PROSPECTS, New York, Basic Books, 1959.

Merton, R. K. SOCIAL CONFLICTS OVER STYLES OF SOCIOLOGICAL WORK, in Transactions of the Fourth World Congress of Sociology, III. Louvain, International Sociological Association, 1959.

Merton, R. K. PARADIGM FOR THE SOCIOLOGY OF KNOWLEDGE, in Social Theory and Social Structure, New York, The Free Press, 1957.

Miller, R. B. INTRODUCTION: RESEARCH SUPPORT AND INTELLECTUAL ADVANCE IN THE SOCIAL SCIENCES, Items, 37:2-3, Sept., 1983, pp. 33-35.

Mills, C. Wright. THE SOCIOLOGICAL IMAGINATION, New York, Oxford University Press, 1959.

Mohan, R. P. and D. Martindale (eds.), HANDBOOK OF COMTEMPORARY DEVELOPMENTS IN WORLD SOCIOLOGY, Westport, CT., Greenwood Press, 1975.

Mohan, R. P. CONTEMPORARY SOCIOLOGY IN INDIA, in Handbook of Contemporary Developments in World Sociology, eds. Mohan R. P. and D. Martindale, Westport, CT., Greenwood, 1975.

Moore, W. E. CAN THE DISCIPLINE SURVIVE ITS PRACTITIONERS?, American Sociologist, 16, 1981, 56-58.

Moore, W. GLOBAL SOCIOLOGY: THE WORLD AS A SINGULAR SYSTEM, American Journal of Sociology, 71, 1966, 475-482.

Morrow, R.A. CRITICAL THEORY AND CRITICAL SOCIOLOGY, Canadian Review of Sociology and Anthropology, 22:5, December, 1985, 710-747.

Moskos, C. C. EMERGING NATIONS AND IDEOLOGIES OF AMERICAN SOCIAL SCIENTISTS, American Sociologist, 2:2, 1967, 67-72.

Motwani, K. (ed.). A CRITIQUE OF EMPIRICISM IN SOCIOLOGY, Delhi, Allied, 1967.

Mukerjee, R. K. PRESIDENTIAL ADDRESS (1958), All India Sociological Conference, in R. N. Saksena (ed.), Sociology, Social Research and Social Problems in India, New York, Asia, 1961.

Mukherjee, R. TRENDS IN INDIAN SOCIOLOGY, Contributions to Indian Sociology, 13:2, July-December, 1979.

Mukherjee, R. TRENDS IN INDIAN SOCIOLOGY, Current Sociology, 25:3, 1977.

Mukherjee, R. THE VALUE-BASE OF SOCIAL ANTHROPOLOGY: THE CONTEXT OF INDIA IN PARTICULAR, Current Anthropology; 17:1, 1976, 71-95.

Mullins, N. C. THEORIES AND THEORY GROUPS REVISITED, in R. Collins (ed.), Sociological Theory, pp. 319-337. San Francisco, Jossey-Bass, 1983.

Mullins, N. C. THEORIES AND THEORY GROUPS IN CONTEMPORARY AMERICAN SOCIOLOGY, New York, Harper and Row, 1973.

Myrdal, G. HOW SCIENTIFIC ARE THE SOCIAL SCIENCES?, Journal of Social Issues, 28:4, 1972, 151-170.

Myrdal, G. OBJECTIVITY AND SOCIAL RESEARCH, London, Duckworth, 1969.

Myrdal, G. THE POLITICAL ELEMENT IN THE DEVELOPMENT OF ECONOMIC THEORY, Cambridge, Harvard University Press, 1965.

Myrdal, G. VALUES IN SOCIAL THEORY, London, Routledge and Kegan Paul, 1958.

Myrdal, G. et al. AN AMERICAN DILEMMA, New York, Harper, 1944.

Naegele, K. D. CANADIAN SOCIETY: SOME REFLECTIONS in B. Blishen et al (eds.), Canadian Society, Toronto, Macmillan, 1961.

Namboodiri, N. K. ON SOCIOLOGY IN INDIA: YESTERDAY, TODAY, AND TOMORROW, Social Forces, 59:1, Sept. 1980, 285-290.

Nandy, S. K. ASPECTS OF DEVELOPMENT OF SOCIOLOGY IN INDIA: A STUDY IN THE SOCIOLOGY OF SOCIOLOGY, in Tiryakian E. A. (ed.), The Phenomenon of Sociology: A Reader in the Sociology of Sociology, pp. 121-145, N.Y. Appleton-Century Crafts, 1971.

Narain, D. FOR A SOCIOLOGY OF INDIA: SOME OBSERVATIONS, Contributions to Indian Sociology, 5, 1971.

Nayar, P. K. B. (ed.). SOCIOLOGY IN INDIA: RETROSPECT AND PROSPECT, Delhi, B. R. Publishing, 1982.

Nettler, G. SOCIOLOGIST AS ADVOCATE, Canadian Journal of Sociology, 5:1, 1980, 31-53.

Nisbet, R. A. THE SOCIAL BOND, New York, Alfred A. Knopf, 1970.

Nisbet, R. A. THE SOCIOLOGICAL TRADITION, New York, Basic Books, 1966.

Oberschall, A. THEORIES OF SOCIAL CONFLICT, Palo Alto, Annual Review of Sociology, 1978.

Olsen, M. E. and M. Micklin (eds.), HANDBOOK OF APPLIED SOCIOLOGY, New York, Praeger, 1981.

Oommen, T. K. SOCIOLOGY IN INDIA: A PLEA FOR CONTEXTUALIZATION, Sociological Bulletin, 32:2, September, 1983, 111-136.

Oommen, T. K. and P. N. Mukherji (eds.), INDIAN SOCIOLOGY: REFLECTIONS AND INTROSPECTIONS, Bombay, Popular, 1986.

O'Neill, J. PHENOMENOLOGICAL SOCIOLOGY, Canadian Review of Sociology and Anthropology, 22:5, December, 1985, 748-770.

Page, C. H. FOREWORD in Hinkle, R. C. and G. J. Hinkle, The Development of Modern Sociology, New York, Random, 1954.

Parsons, T. ON BUILDING SOCIAL SYSTEM THEORY: A PERSONAL HISTORY, Daedalus, 9g, 1970, 826-881.

Parsons, T. EVALUATION AND OBJECTIVITY IN SOCIAL SCIENCE: AN INTERPRETATION OF MAX WEBER'S CONTRIBUTIONS, in Sociological Theory and Modern Society, New York, The Free Press, 1968.

Parsons, T. (ed.). AMERICAN SOCIOLOGY, New York, Basic Books, 1968.

Parsons, T. SOME PROBLEMS CONFRONTING SOCIOLOGY AS A PROFESSION, American Sociological Review, 24:547-559, 1959.

Parsons, T. AN APPROACH TO THE SOCIOLOGY OF KNOWLEDGE, in Transactions of the Fourth World Congress of Sociology, IV, Louvain, International Sociological Association, 1959a.
Pease, J. et al. IDEOLOGICAL CURRENTS IN AMERICAN STRATIFICATION LITERATURE, American Sociologist, 5:2, 1970, 127-137.

Pinto, D. (ed.). CONTEMPORARY ITALIAN SOCIOLOGY, New York, Cambridge University Press, 1981.

Poloma, M. M. CONTEMPORARY SOCIOLOGICAL THEORY, New York, Macmillan, 1979.

Porter, J. THE MEASURE OF CANADIAN SOCIETY, Toronto, Gage, 1979.

Preston, R. A. (ed.). PERSPECTIVES ON REVOLUTION AND EVOLUTION, Durham, N. C., Duke University Press, 1979.

Rabow, J. and L. G. Zucker. WHITHER SOCIOLOGY, Sociology and Social Research, 65:1, 10-22.

Ramu, G. N. and S. Johnson (eds.). TOWARDS A CANADIAN SOCIOLOGY, in Introduction to Canadian Society, Toronto, Macmillan of Canada, 1976.

Rao, M. S. A. et al. REPORT ON THE STATUS OF TEACHING OF SOCIOLOGY AND SOCIAL ANTHROPOLOGY, Part I, Recommendations, New Delhi, University Grants Commission, 1978.

Rao, S.V.V.S. and C.R.P. Rao. REFLEXIONS ON THE CRISIS OF INDIAN SOCIOLOGY, Sociological Bulletin, 26:2, 1977.

Reiss, A. J. PUTTING SOCIOLOGY INTO POLICY, Social Problems, 17:3, Winter 1970, 289-294.

Reiss, A. J. WHITHER THE CRAFT, Sociological Inquiry, 39:2, Spring 1969, 149-154.

Restivo, S. THE MYTH OF THE KUHNIAN REVOLUTION, in R. Collins (ed.), Sociological Theory, pp. 293-305, San Francisco, Jossey-Bass, 1983.

Rex, J. BRITISH SOCIOLOGY 1960-80 - AN ESSAY, Social Forces, 61:4, June 1983, 999-1009.

Rex, J. THE CONCEPT OF RACE IN SOCIOLOGICAL THEORY, in Stone, J. (ed.), Race, Ethnicity, and Social Change, pp. 44-58, North Scituate, Duxbury Press, 1977.

Reynolds, L. J. and J. M. Reynolds (ed.), THE SOCIOLOGY OF SOCIOLOGY, New York, David McKay, 1970.

Richardson, J. R. and B. Wellman. STRUCTURAL ANALYSIS, Canadian Review of Sociology and Anthropology, 22:5, December, 1985, 771-793.

Riecken, H. W. THE NATIONAL SCIENCE FOUNDATION AND THE SOCIAL SCIENCES, Items, 37:2-3, Sept. 1983, pp. 39-42.

Riley, G. PARTISANSHIP AND OBJECTIVITY IN THE SOCIAL SCIENCES, American Sociologist, 6:1, 1971, 6-12.

Ritzer, G. SOCIOLOGICAL THEORY, New York, Alfred Knopf, 1983.

Ritzer, G. TOWARD AN INTEGRATED SOCIOLOGICAL PARADIGM, Boston, Allyn and Baron, 1981.

Ritzer, G. TOWARD AN INTEGRATED SOCIOLOGICAL PARADIGM, in Snizek, W. E. et al (eds.), Contemporary Issues in Theory and Method, Westport, CT. Greenwood, 1979.

Ritzer, G. SOCIOLOGY: A MULTIPLE PARADIGM SCIENCE, American Sociologist, 10, 1975, 156-67.

Roach, J. L. and J. D. Colfax. RADICAL SOCIOLOGY, New York, Basic Books, 1971.

Robinson, M. THE ROLE OF THE PRIVATE FOUNDATIONS,Items, 37:2-3, Sept. 1983, pp. 35-39.

Rocher, G. THE FUTURE OF SOCIOLOGY IN CANADA, in C. Beattie and S. Crysdale (eds.), Sociology Canada: Readings, 484-493, Toronto, Butterworths, 1977.

Rocher, G. A GENERAL INTRODUCTION TO SOCIOLOGY: A THEORETICAL PERSPECTIVE, Toronto, Macmillan, 1972.

Rose, A. M. HINDU VALUES AND INDIAN SOCIAL PROBLEMS, Sociological Quarterly, 8, Summer 1967, 329-339.

Rose, A. SOCIOLOGY AND THE STUDY OF VALUES, British Journal of Sociology, 9, 1956, 1-18.

Rossi, P. H. THE CHALLENGE AND OPPORTUNITIES OF APPLIED SOCIAL RESEARCH, American Sociological Review, 45, 1980, 889-904.

Rotestein, A, and G. Lax FACULTY CITIZENSHIP IN CANADIAN UNIVERSITIES in Getting It Back: A Program for Canadian Independence, edited by A. Rotestein and G. Lax, pp. 193-205. Toronto, Clarke Irwin, 1974.

Roucek, J. S. (ed.). READINGS IN CONTEMPORARY AMERICAN SOCIOLOGY, New York, Philosophical Library, 1958.

Saksena, R. N. SOME OBSERVATIONS ON SOCIOLOGY IN INDIA, American Sociological Review, 27, 1962, 95-98.

Saksena, R. N. (ed.). SOCIOLOGY, SOCIAL RESEARCH AND SOCIAL PROBLEMS IN INDIA, New York, Asia, 1961.
Saran, A. K. SOCIOLOGY IN INDIA, in Roucek, J. S. (ed.), Contemporary Sociology, New York, Philosophical Library, 1958.

Scheler, M. PROBLEMS OF A SOCIOLOGY OF KNOWLEDGE, Boston, Routledge, 1980.

Schervish, P. G. THE LABELING PERSPECTIVE: ITS BIAS AND POTENTIAL IN THE STUDY OF POLITICAL DEVIANCE, American Sociologist, 8:2, 1973, 47-56.

Schuessler, K. F. QUANTITATIVE METHODOLOGY IN SOCIOLOGY: THE LAST 25 YEARS, American Behavioral Scientist, 23:6, 1980, 835-860.

Schuessler, K. SOCIOLOGY TOWARD THE YEAR 2000, Society, July-August, 1979, 31-35.

Sharma, S. L. WESTERN THEORY AND INDIAN REALITY: THE QUESTION OF
   RELEVANCE, paper presented at the 10th World Congress of
   Sociology, Mexico City, August, 1982.

Sherman, H. J. and J. L. Wood. SOCIOLOGY: TRADITIONAL AND
   RADICAL PERSPECTIVES, New York, Harper and Row, 1979.

Shils, E. THE ACADEMIC PROFESSION IN INDIA, Minerva, Sept. 1979,
   356.

Shils, E. TRADITION, ECOLOGY, AND INSTITUTION IN THE HISTORY OF
   SOCIOLOGY, Daedalus, 99, 1970: 760-825.

Short, J. F. (ed.). THE STATE OF SOCIOLOGY: PROBLEMS AND
   PROSPECTS, Beverly Hills, Sage, 1981.

Sibley, E. THE EDUCATION OF SOCIOLOGISTS IN THE UNITED STATES,
   New York, Russell Sage, 1963.

Sieber, J. E. INTRODUCTION: CRUCIAL VALUE ISSUES FOR APPLIED
   SOCIAL SCIENTISTS, American Behavioral Scientist, 26:2, 1982,
   149-158.

Singh Y. INDIAN SOCIOLOGY: SOCIAL CONDITIONING AND EMERGING
   CONCERNS, New Delhi, Vistar, 1986.

Singh, Y. ON THE HISTORY OF SOCIOLOGY IN INDIA, in M. Mullick
   (ed.) - Social Inquiry: Goals and Approaches, pp. 107-126, New
   Delhi, Manohar, 1979.

Singh, Y. FOR A SOCIOLOGY OF INDIA, Contributions to Indian
   Sociology, 4, 1970.

Singh, Y. SOCIOLOGY FOR INDIA: THE EMERGING PERSPECTIVE, in
   Unnithan et al (eds.), Sociology for India, New Delhi,
   Prentice-Hall, 1967.

Sjoberg, G. (ed.). ETHICS, POLITICS, AND SOCIAL RESEARCH,
   Cambridge, Schenkman, 1967.

Skidmore, W. THEORETICAL THINKING IN SOCIOLOGY, New York,
   Cambridge University Press, 1975.

Smelser, N. J. (ed.). SOCIOLOGY, Englewood Cliffs, N.J.,
   Prentice-Hall, 1969.

Snizek, W. E. et al (eds.). CONTEMPORARY ISSUES IN THEORY AND
   RESEARCH: A METASOCIOLOGICAL PERSPECTIVE, Westport, CT.
   Greenwood Press, 1979.

Social Science Federation of Canada SEX BIAS IN RESEARCH: CURRENT AWARENESS AND STRATEGIES TO ELIMINATE BIAS WITHIN CANADIAN SOCIAL SCIENCES, Ottawa, Social Science Federation of Canada, 1974.

Sorokin, P. A. FADS AND FOIBLES IN MODERN SOCIOLOGY, Chicago, Regnery, 1956.

Srinivas, M. N. ITINERARIES OF AN INDIAN SOCIAL ANTHROPOLOGIST, International Social Science Journal, 25:1-2, 1973, 129-148.

Srivastava, R. N. SOCIOLOGY FOR INDIA: SOME CONSIDERATIONS, Indian Journal of Social Research, 7:3, 1966:198-205.

Stehr, N. and L. E. Larson. THE RISE AND DECLINE OF AREAS OF SPECIALIZATION, American Sociologist, 7:1972.

Stein, M. and A. Vidich (eds.). SOCIOLOGY ON TRIAL, Englewood Cliffs, Prentice-Hall, 1963.

Stolte Heiskanen, V. THE MYTH OF THE MIDDLE-CLASS FAMILY IN AMERICAN FAMILY SOCIOLOGY, American Sociology, 6:1, 1971, 14-18.

Stone, J. RACE RELATIONS AND THE SOCIOLOGICAL TRADITION, in Race, Ethnicity, and Social Change, pp. 59-74, North Scitrate, Duxbury Press, 1977.

Stolzman, J. and H. Gamberg. THE NATIONAL QUESTION AND CANADIAN SOCIOLOGY, Canadian Journal of Sociology, 1975, 1:91-106.

Strasser, H. THE NORMATIVE STRUCTURE OF SOCIOLOGY, London, Routledge and Kegan Paul, 1976.

Street, D. P. and E. A. Weinstein. PROBLEMS AND PROSPECTS OF APPLIED SOCIOLOGY, American Sociologist, 10, 1975, 65-72.

Suda, J. P. THE TEACHING OF SOCIOLOGY IN INDIA, Indian Journal of Social Research, 8:1, 1967.

Swedberg, Richard. COMMUNISM IN NORTH AMERICAN SOCIOLOGY: A STUDY OF THE RELATIONSHIP BETWEEN POLITICAL COMMITMENT AND SOCIAL THEORY, American Sociologist, 15:232-246, 1980.

Szymanski, A. TOWARD A RADICAL SOCIOLOGY, in J. D. Colfax (ed.), Radical Sociology, New York, Basic Books, 1971.

Thio, A. CLASS BIAS IN THE SOCIOLOGY OF DEVIANCE, American Sociologist, 8:1, 1973, 1-12.

Tibbets, P. THE POSITIVISM-HUMANISM DEBATE IN SOCIOLOGY: A RECONSIDERATION, Sociological Inquiry, 52:3, 1982, 184-199.

Tiryakian, E.A. SOCIOLOGY'S GREAT LEAP FORWARD: THE CHALLENGE OF INTERNATIONALISATION, International Sociology, 1:2, June 1986, 155-171.

Tiryakian, E. A. THE SIGNIFICANCE OF SCHOOLS IN THE DEVELOPMENT OF SOCIOLOGY, in Snizek et al (eds.), Contemporary Issues in Theory and Method, Westport, CT., Greenwood, 1979.

Tiryakian, E. A. (ed.). THE PHENOMENON OF SOCIOLOGY, New York, Appleton-Century-Crofts, 1971.

Turner, J. H. THE STRUCTURE OF SOCIOLOGICAL THEORY, Homewood, Dorsey Press, 1982.

Uberoi, J.P.S. SCIENCE AND SWARAJ, Contributions to Indian Sociology, 2, New Series, 1968.

Ujjar, Singh. NEW HORIZONS IN TEACHING AND RESEARCH IN SOCIOLOGY IN INDIA, Indian Journal of Social Research, 23:1, 71-79, April 1982.

Unnithan, T.K.N. et al (eds.). SOCIOLOGY FOR INDIA, New Delhi, Prentice-Hall, 1967.

Useem, M. GOVERNMENT INFLUENCE ON THE SOCIAL SCIENCE PARADIGM, Sociological Quarterly 17:146-161, 1971.

Valee, F. G. and D. R. Whyte. CANADIAN SOCIETY: TRENDS AND PERSPECTIVES in B. R. Blishen et al (eds.), Canadian Society: Sociological Perspectives, Toronto, Macmillan, 1968.

Valien, P. and B. Valien. GENERAL SOCIOLOGICAL THEORIES OF CURRENT REFERENCE, in H. Becker and H. Boskoff (eds.), Modern Sociological Theory, New York, Holt, Rinehart and Winston, 1957.

Varma, S. C. SOCIAL INQUIRY FOR WHAT?, in M. Mullick (ed.), Social Enquiry: Goals and Approaches, pp. 89-105, New Delhi, Manohar, 1979.

Vidich, A. J. and S. M. Lyman. AMERICAN SOCIOLOGY: WORLDLY REJECTIONS OF RELIGION AND THEIR DIRECTIONS, New Haven, Yale University Press, 1985.

Walker, A. J. and L. Thompson. FEMINISM AND FAMILY STUDIES, Journal of Family Issues 5:6, December 1984, 545-570.

Wallace, R. A. CONTEMPORARY SOCIOLOGICAL THEORY, Englewood Cliffs, N.J., Prentice-Hall, 1980.

Walsh, D. VARIETIES OF POSITIVISM, in P. Filmer et al, New Directions in Sociological Theory, Cambridge, Mass., MIT Press, 1972.

Wardell M. L. and E. R. Fuhrman. CONTROVERSY AND IDEOLOGICAL HEGEMONY IN SOCIOLOGICAL THEORY, Sociological Quarterly, 22, 1981:479-493.

Watson, G. L. THE POVERTY OF SOCIOLOGY IN A CHANGING SOCIETY, Canadian Journal of Sociology, 1:3, 345-362, 1975.

Weber, M. THE METHODOLOGY OF THE SOCIAL SCIENCES, New York, Free Press, 1949.

Weber, Max. SCIENCE AS A VOCATION, in H. H. Gerth and C. Wright Mills (eds.). From Max Weber: Essays in Sociology, pp. 129-156, New York, Oxford University Press, 1946.

Weber, Max. POLITICS AS A VOCATION, in H. H. Gerth and C. Wright Mills (eds.). From Max Weber: Essays in Sociology, pp. 77-128, New York, Oxford University Press, 1946.

Webber, I. L. SOCIOLOGY: PAROCHIAL OR UNIVERSAL? Social Forces, 60:2, December 1981, 416-431.

Weiner, M. SOCIAL SCIENCE RESEARCH AND PUBLIC POLICY IN INDIA, Economic and Political Weekly, September 1979, pp. 1579-874, 1622-28.

Weiss, C. H. and M. J. Bucuvalas. THE CHALLENGE OF SOCIAL RESEARCH TO DECISION MAKING, in C. H. Weiss (ed.), Using Social Research in Public Policy Making, Lexington, Mass., Lexington Books, 1977, 213-34.

Weller, L. SOCIOLOGY IN ISRAEL, Westport, CT., Greenwood, 1974.

Wells, R. H. and J. S. Picori. AMERICAN SOCIOLOGY: THEORETICAL AND METHODOLOGICAL STRUCTURE, Washington, D.C., University Press of America, 1981.

Whyte, D. R. SOCIOLOGY AND THE NATIONALIST CHALLENGE IN CANADA, paper presented at the 10th World Congress of Sociology, Mexico, August, 1982.

Wiley, N. THE RISE AND FALL OF DOMINATING THEORIES IN AMERICAN SOCIOLOGY, in Contemporary Issues in Theory and Research, (ed.), W. Snizek et al, Westport, Greenwood, 1979.

Wilson, E. K. SOCIOLOGY: RULES, ROLES AND RELATIONSHIPS, Homewood, The Dursey Press, 1971.

Wilson, E. O. SOCIOBIOLOGY: THE NEW SYNTHESIS, Cambridge, Mass., Harvard University Press, 1975.

Wolff, K. H. (ed.); FROM KARL MANNHEIM, New York, Oxford University Press,1971.

Wolff, K. H. THE SOCIOLOGY OF KNOWLEDGE AND SOCIOLOGICAL THEORY, in L. Gross (ed.), Symposium on Sociological Theory, New York, Harper and Row, 1959.

Wolff, K. NOTES TOWARD A SOCIO-CULTURAL INTERPRETATION OF AMERICAN SOCIOLOGY, American Sociological Review, 11, 1946:545-553.

Yamagishi, T. and M. C. Brinton. SOCIOLOGY IN JAPAN AND SHAKAI-ISHIKIRON, American Sociologist, 1980, 15, 192-207.

Zeitlin, I. M. IDEOLOGY AND THE DEVELOPMENT OF SOCIOLOGICAL THEORY, Englewood Cliffs, N.J., Prentice-Hall, 1968.

Zelditch, M. DO MULTIPLE STRATEGIES CONVERGE? Society, July/August, 1979, 25-30.

Zetterberg, H. L. (ed.). SOCIOLOGY IN THE UNITED STATES OF AMERICA: A TREND REPORT, Westport CT., Greenwood Press, 1956, Reprint, 1973.

Zimmerman, C. C. CONTEMPORARY TRENDS IN SOCIOLOGY IN AMERICA AND ABROAD, in J. S. Roucek (ed.), Readings in Contemporary American Sociology, pp. 3-25, New York, Philosophical Library, 1958.

Znaniecki, F. THE SOCIAL ROLE OF THE MAN OF KNOWLEDGE, New York, Columbia University Press, 1940.

INDEX

Abrams, P 35
Adams, B.N. 23
Ahmed, I. 57
American, ix
American Sociology, 3, 13,
15-36; Impact on India,
50-51, 53-55; impact on
Canada, 72-73; future of
104-105
American textbooks, ix
Anderson, A.A. 35, 103
Antonio, R.J. 32
Aron, R. 99
Atal, Y. 4, 48-49, 56
Baily, F.G. 55-56
Baldock, C.V. 35, 98
Barnes, H.E. 40
Beattie and Crysdale, 66
Ben-David, J. 3
Becker, H. 8, 25, 30, 33
Berger, P. 81
Bierstedt, R. 3, 15, 108
Birnbaum, N. 35
Blau, P. 26
Blummer, H. 26
Bogardus, E.S. 17-18
Bombay, University of, ix, 38,
47
Bottomore, T.B. 40-41, 101
Brooks, H. 89
Brym, R.J. 35
Burr, W.R. 33
Calcutta, University of 38
Canada, ix-x, 1, 61 ff
Canadian Journal of Sociology,
68
Canadian Review of Sociology
and Anthropology, 68
Canadian Sociology and
Anthropology Association,
68
Canadian Sociology 61-79;
French Canadian Sociology
62-64; English Canadian
Sociology 64-69;
Comparison with Indian
Sociology, 69-70;
Canadianization movement,
76-81; relevant, 89; future

of, 103-104
Castells, E. 33
Chekki, D.A. 35, 41, 45, 97
Clark, S.D. 9, 35, 65, 70, 72
Clement, W. 74, 76, 78, 94,
104
Clinard, M.B. 35, 40, 54, 97,
102
Coburn, D. 68, 98, 100
Conflict theory, 23-25
Conner, D.M. 66-67, 97
Coser, L.A. 3, 31-32, 109
Crook, R.K.N. 78
Cross-national reasearch ix-x,
109
Curtis, J.E. 8, 15, 66-67, 97
Damle, Y.B. 38, 55, 103
Davis, A.K. 66, 69, 72
Dawson, C.A. 65
Dependency theory, 4, 109
Desai, A.R. 9, 38
Desai, I.P. 38, 50
Domain assumptions, 12
Dube, S.C. 38, 59
Dumont, L. 55
Durkheim, E. ix, 34
Eichler, M. 79
Eisenstadt, S.N. 22
Elder, J.W. 35, 40, 54, 97,
102
Elkin, F. 62
Ethical context, 2
Ehtical dilemma, x
Ethnomethodoloby, 26
Europe, 7
Exchange theory, 26
Fact-value controversy, ix, 81
ff.
Faris, R.E.L. 53
Forcese, D. 35, 64, 97, 103
Friederichs, R.W. 2-3, 8, 15,
29, 91, 93, 97
Fuhrman, E. 1981
Gamberg, H. 9, 35, 70-72, 74
Gamson, W. 87
Gardezi, H.N. 98
Garfinkel, H. 26
Geddes, P. 38
Ghurye, G.S. 38-39, 47

ABOUT THE AUTHOR

DAN A. CHEKKI is a Professor of Sociology and has taught at the University of Winnipeg since 1968. Earlier (1958-1968) he taught sociology at the Universities of Bombay and Karnatak. His numerous research papers in the areas of social change, sociology of the family, urban community and development have appeared in various professional journals and books. Professor Chekki has been secretary of the International Sociological Association, Committee on Community Research. He is an associate editor of the **Journal of Comparative Family Studies** and Editor of the **Library of Sociology** series, Garland Publishing, New York and London. Dr Chekki's publications include **Modernization and Kin Network, The Sociology of Contemporary India**, Community Development: Theory and Method of Planned Change, and Participatory Democracy in Action.